This sewing dictionary has been compiled by Perivale-Gütermann Limited, the well-known sewing thread company, part of the international Gütermann Group of Companies, to help you with your dressmaking. It contains lots of handy hints and instructions, explained carefully and illustrated with over 300 clear diagrams and photographs.

Whether you are learning dressmaking at school, college or at home, you will find this a useful reference book to own. Keep it always within reach (your sewing table or sewing box) and just look up anything you're not quite sure of—in the long run, it will save you a great deal of time, effort and work.

Gütermann
Sewing A-Z

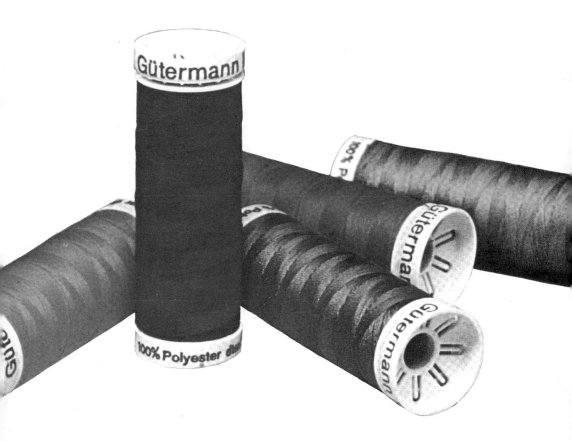

First published in Germany as the *Gütermann Näh-Lexikon*.
This edition published by
Perivale-Gütermann Limited, Wadsworth Road,
Greenford, Middlesex, UB6 7JS

First printed 1972
Reprinted 1972
Revised 1979

© Perivale-Gütermann Limited 1972

ISBN 0 263 05019 X

Made and printed in Great Britain by
Morrison & Gibb Limited, London and Edinburgh

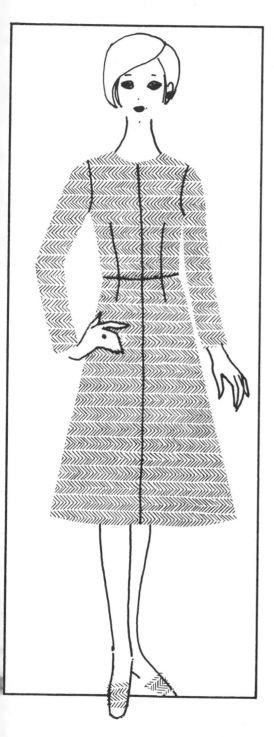

This first section (pages i to xii) has been included here for your use as a step by step guide when using a basic paper pattern. It also refers you to the appropriate part of the A-Z section (pages 5 to 136) where and when necessary. We have anticipated that you will wish to make your own notes and have left pages 1 to 4 blank for this purpose.

A basic pattern consists of the necessary pattern pieces to make a plain, fitted dress with a figure-hugging bodice, a slightly flared skirt and narrow, set-in sleeves.

Each pattern piece is cut to body proportions, which makes it easy to adapt to personal measurements.

Once a basic pattern has been made to correspond to personal requirements, it becomes a useful guide for cutting out simple garments, such as skirts, plain blouses and dresses, overalls and even collarless coats. More importantly though, it serves to correct the measurements of other bought patterns.

To obtain a personalised basic pattern, use a bought pattern from a paper pattern catalogue in the style shown in the sketch and in the nearest stock size. Then personal measurements have to be taken with care and may be entered in the section for measurements in this book (see MEASUREMENTS, HOW TO TAKE, page 68). These are compared to the measurements of the pattern and any variations can then be made accordingly. Use the instruction shown in this book (see PATTERN ADJUSTMENTS, page 85).

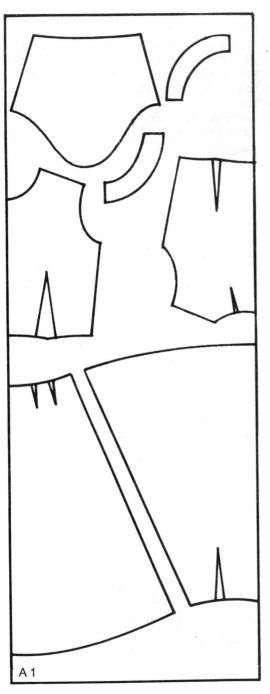

A 1

To make sure that the pattern is now figure correct, it should be tested by using it to cut out a garment in inexpensive fabric, such as cotton calico or lining material. This will provide a perfect fitting guide or an underdress which may come in useful later.

Any alteration made during fitting should also be transferred to the pattern. Once the basic pattern has passed its figure test, it will be ready to help to make many well-fitting garments and add to the joy of dressmaking.

Cutting

The following equipment is required for cutting out and tacking:

one pair of large, sharp scissors, pins, tailor's chalk and yard stick
tape measure
dressmaker's tracing paper
tracing wheel
fine handsewing needles
tacking thread
and a well-fitting thimble.

(For other tools see TOOLS FOR DRESSMAKING, page 128.)

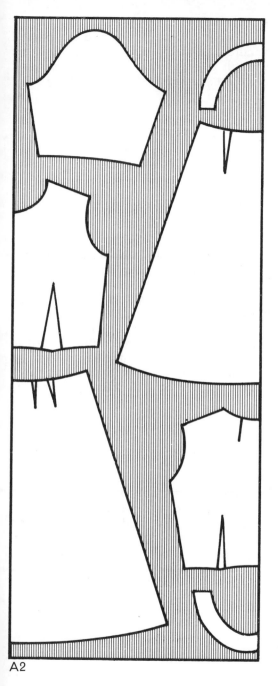

A2

A1

Before cutting, fold the fabric in half lengthwise and lay it flat on a large table. For fabrics without surface interest, the pattern pieces are laid on in the order shown (Fig. A1). This makes economical use of the length.

To make sure that the finished garment hangs well it is important to cut the sections in the straight of the fabric grain, unless shown otherwise.

Most pattern pieces are cut out double and the centre front lines of the bodice and the skirt are cut on the fold.

A2

Fabrics with a one-way design or nap, such as velvet, face cloth or cord, are cut out in the direction of the design or nap (Fig. A2).

Stripes or checks which require matching to allow the design to meet perfectly in the seam lines, need to be cut out with particular care. Matching may require a little more fabric which should be thought of at the time of purchase (see CUTTING, page 28).

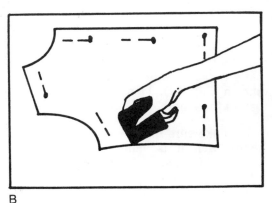

B

B

The pattern pieces should be pinned securely to the fabric, and for patterns without seam allowances, the edges and darts are marked first before cutting.

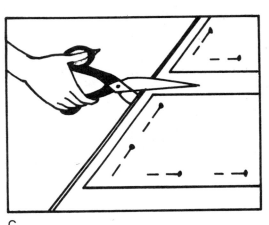

C

C

Seam allowance widths are cut the same for all matching seams. (Seam allowance is the amount added to the pattern outline to facilitate stitching the sections together.) Add $\frac{1}{2}''$ to $\frac{3}{4}''$ (1 to $1\frac{1}{2}$ cm) to the armhole line, the top of the sleeves and the neckline, $\frac{3}{4}''$ to $1\frac{1}{4}''$ (2 to 3 cm) to shoulder, waistline and sleeves, and $1\frac{1}{2}''$ (4 cm) to side seams and centre back seam. Allow 2″ to 3″ (5 to 8 cm) for turning up the hem.

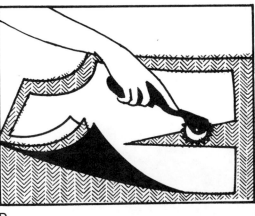

D

D

Underlay the cut out sections with tracing paper and using the tracing wheel, trace the outline of the darts and the pattern edges to the corresponding, opposite side of the fabric. Heavy fabrics are marked more easily with tailor's tacks (see TAILOR'S TACKS, page 127).

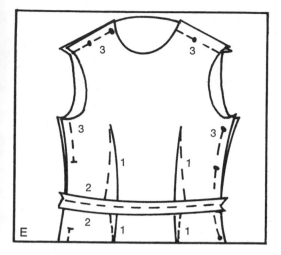

Tacking

Seam edges may be neatened carefully after cutting and sections are then pinned together on the wrong side.

E

Firstly pin and tack all darts, and then matching the waistline darts in the bodice and the skirt, pin and tack the waist seam line. Finally pin and tack the shoulder and side seams (see BASTING, page 7).

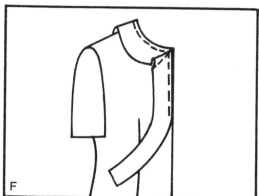

F

To strengthen the neckline and hemline edge in fine fabrics, tack a strip of taffeta, fine cotton or Vilene into position (or refer to STIFFENING AND BACKING (page 125) for other styles).

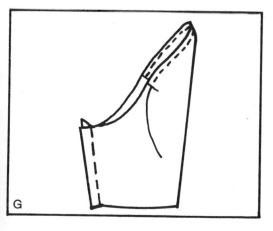

G

Tack the sleeve seams and ease in the fullness around the top with small running stitches, between the markings shown on the pattern.

Lightly press the tacked seams to allow the garment to be fitted properly.

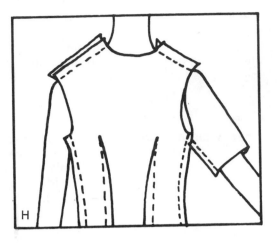

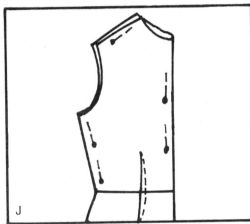

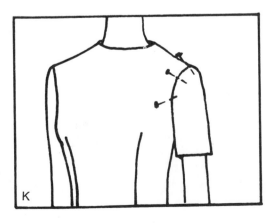

1st fitting

H

It is easier to start fitting a garment by putting it on inside out. Alterations to darts and seams can then be pinned following the tacked seam lines. If letting out is necessary, the tacking thread can be removed quickly for re-pinning.

J

After this the garment is put on right side out. Alterations made at this fitting are on the outside and have to be traced through to the inside.

K

Sleeves are only pinned into position for the 1st fitting.

Stitching

Equipment required for stitching and pressing:

sewing machine (swing needle if possible).
Gütermann Sew-all thread for stitching
Gütermann Twist for buttonholes and decorative effects
iron with thermostatic control
ironing board with adjustable feet
sleeve board with removable cover
two pieces of cloth for pressing
hemguide to mark a straight hemline, preferable for use without assistance
unpicking knife

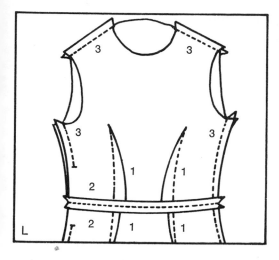

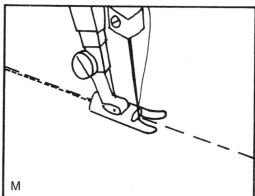

L

The sequence used for stitching is the same as for tacking: first the darts (1), then joining the bodice sections to the skirt sections (2), and finally the shoulder and side seams (3) (see TOP-STITCHING AND QUILTING, page 130).

M

Seams should be stitched closely to the line of tacking stitches, and to save time a number of seams may be stitched before pressing. Remember to remove the tacking threads first and that some parts of the garment can be reached more easily with the iron before all the sections are stitched together.

N

After the sleeve seams have been stitched and pressed, the lower sleeve edges are finished. Attach shirt cuffs, turn-up facing or other finishes. Next sleeves should be tacked into the armholes and the zip fastener tacked into the opening.

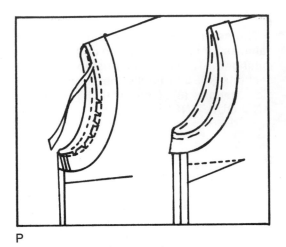

P

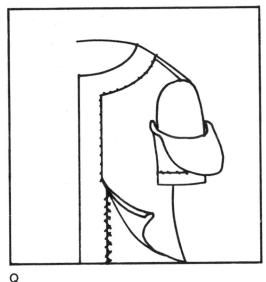

Q

2nd fitting

O

This fitting is especially designed for checking the correct sit of the sleeves and the length of the skirt (see FITTING, page 42).

Finishing

P

On sleeveless dresses, armhole edges are faced with bias or shaped facings (see ASSEMBLING GARMENT SECTIONS, page 6). Otherwise the sleeves are then stitched into the armholes (see SLEEVES, HOW TO SET IN GARMENT, page 120) and the zip fastener stitched into the opening (see ZIP FASTENER, page 135). Finally the hem is turned up and handsewn into position (see HEMS, page 55) and the dress is pressed for final finish.

The dress is finished now but it has no lining. For woollen or fine fabrics a lining is, however, advisable.

Q

The lining should be cut the same as the dress and assembled and stitched in the same order. Lining seams should face into the dress (see LININGS, page 64 and LININGS FOR SKIRTS, page 65).

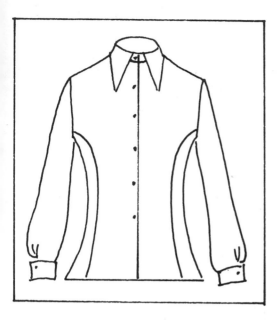

Blouses

Stitch sidebust and waistline darts in blouse front (see DARTS, page 31).

Arrange front fastening.

Join front and back to stitch shoulder and side seams.

Neaten seam allowances (see SEAM FINISHES, page 110).

Make collar and attach to neckline (see COLLARS, page 21).

Stitch and finish sleeves. Attach cuffs, stitch sleeves into armholes (see SLEEVES, HOW TO SET IN GARMENT, page 120).

Make narrow hem on lower edge or, as for jumpers, turn up wider hem and hand-sew as required for fabric type.

Make buttonholes and sew on buttons (see BUTTONHOLES, page 17 and BUTTONS, page 19).

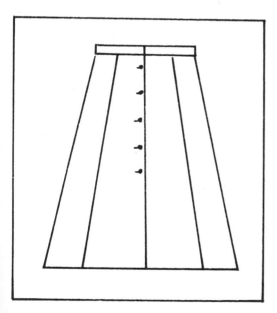

Skirts

Stitch darts in skirt front and back (see DARTS, page 31). Pleat or top-stitch as necessary (see PLEATS, page 96 and PLEATED SKIRTS, page 94).

Match and stitch panels together and leave opening in left side or centre back seam.

Sew zip fastener into opening (see ZIP FASTENER, page 135).

Stitch lining sections and leave opening in lower side seams for ease of movement. Turn up lining hem, attach backing for Dior Pleat if used (see DIOR SLIT, page 33).

Slip lining into skirt (see LININGS FOR SKIRTS, page 65).

Attach waistband to skirt waistline (see WAISTBAND FOR SKIRTS AND SLACKS, page 134).

Neaten seams and finish hem (see HEMS, page 55).

Hems in machine or hand-pleated skirts with straight pleats are made up before pleating.

Coats and Jackets

Stitch darts in front sections (see DARTS, page 31).

Interface front edges (see NECK OPENINGS, page 72).

Make bound buttonholes (see BUTTONHOLES, page 17) and stitch on facings (see FACINGS FOR FRONT CLOSINGS, page 39).

Open buttonholes through facings and hem into position.

Make pockets (see POCKETS, page 97).

Stitch back sections together.

Stitch shoulder and side seams, holding in ease or making small dart in back shoulder seam.

Interface collar (see COLLARS, page 21). Stitch sleeves (see SLEEVES, THE CONSTRUCTION OF, page 118). Interface sleeve hemline and turn up hem allowance. Herringbone into position.

Attach collar, set in sleeves (see SLEEVES, HOW TO SET IN GARMENT, page 120).

Turn up coat hem allowance and hand-sew in position (see HEMS, page 55).

Sew in lining and attach buttons (see BUTTONS, page 19).

Making children's clothes

Use the same sequence as shown for making clothes for adults, except for cutting, when wider seam allowances should be cut on. This depends on the fabric but $\frac{3}{4}''$ to $1\frac{1}{4}''$ (2 to 3 cm) are recommended for all edges. An extra deep hem allowance may be stitched in decorative tucks around the outside of the hemline, or turned under twice.

Allow $1\frac{1}{2}''$ (4 cm) on the bodice waistline edge.

Additional seam and hem allowances provide the scope for making garment larger later on.

Additional length for trousers should be allowed on the waistline edge and at the trouser-leg hemline. Decorative braces may be used to hold up the waistline, which can be let down as the child grows. Hip and waistline circumferences in children do not usually increase rapidly.

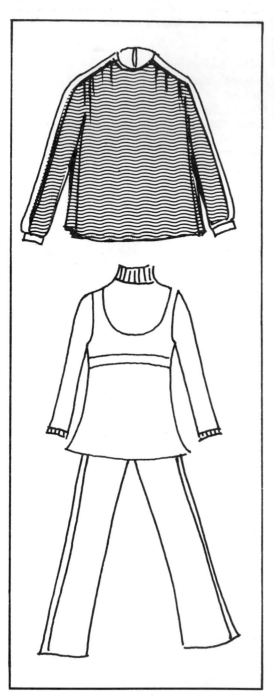

Letting out and lengthening of children's clothes

Any gathers in skirts and bodices can be let out. Smocking too can be unpicked at the sides to provide extra width, leaving only small sections in the centre in groups of pleats.

The depth of pleats in pleated skirts can be reduced or they can be let out completely from the sides of a skirt, leaving flat panels.

Shoulder and bodice sections in plain, coloured dresses can be widened by inserting decorative or contrasting bands. The bodice is cut through from the centre of the shoulders to the waistline on each side and the bands are then stitched into the openings.

Sleeves too can be cut through from the top to the wrist and widened by inserting bands. They can also be lengthened by inserting horizontal bands.

A false hem is usually a final means to lengthen a skirt. The edge of the hemline on a short dress may also be trimmed with a band to match the top.

Trousers can be lengthened attractively with a knitted yoke from the waistline and the hemline of the trouser legs may be gathered into matching, knitted cuffs.

To let out the side seams, a straight band may be inserted from the waistline to the hem.

Fig. 1

Fig. 2

Appliqué

Appliqué is the method of applying a decorative piece of fabric to a second fabric (Fig. 1). The quickest way to apply the appliqué is with an embroidery stitch (i.e. zigzag stitch) using a simple motif and close stitches. Cut out the motifs allowing a small seam allowance. Apply motifs with a machine embroidery stitch. Trim seam allowance close to the line of stitching. Machine-stitch over raw edge of seam line with a close zigzag or satin stitch. For a raised effect, carry a thread under the embroidery stitch (Fig. 2).

Arrowhead or Sprat Head Tacks

These are used to secure the top of a pleat in a narrow skirt, or at the ends of pockets. Mark the arrowhead shape with basting thread.

On some fabrics, marking with chalk is sufficient. Work arrowhead with Güter-mann Twist. Stitches must be placed close together, so that the arrowhead is completely filled with thread when completed. The illustration opposite shows how to work the sprat heads and the arrowhead tacks (Fig. 3 a and b).

For the sprat head tack, insert the needle at the lower right-hand corner, taking a stitch diagonal to each point of the triangle. Continue in this manner until all the space is filled.

For the arrowhead tack, start at the left-hand corner, make a small stitch at the top of the triangle and bring the needle down to the right-hand corner. Continue until the triangle is filled.

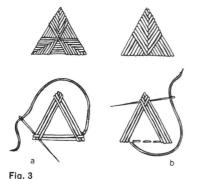

a   b

Fig. 3

Assembling Garment Sections

Between the first and the second fitting, nearly all necessary work on your garment should be completed, so that you have a better picture of how the garment will look when completed. It is a good idea to use a step-by-step guide to assemble a garment: see the twelve rules on how to assemble a garment below.

After the first fitting: Mark alterations with thread you have previously marked with pins during your first fitting. If you have an average figure, corrections are made on the right side of garment only, therefore you have to undo garment sections in order to transfer corrections to the left side of your garment. If your figure is not well proportioned, make alterations on both sides of the garment during the fitting. Stitch darts before basting bodice sections together. It is advisable to remove tailor's tacks before machine-stitching seams. After stitching seams basting thread should be cut every few inches and removed carefully. Press seam open. Repeat this process with each new seam. Pressing is as important as sewing. After you have basted shoulder and side seams, machine-stitch permanently.

Now complete front opening. Sew up buttonholes, using Gütermann Twist, with small herring-bone stitches before pressing.

Stitch all skirt seams and baste skirt to bodice. Stitch waistline seam and press open.

12 rules on how to assemble a garment

1. Pin and baste darts, pin and baste sections of garment together.
2. First fitting. Pin alterations.
3. Undo garment sections again.
4. Transfer alterations to the other side of the garment.

5. Stitch darts, then shoulder and side seams, remove tailor's tacks beforehand.
6. Make buttonholes.
7. Stitch seams of skirt.
8. Complete sleeves, collar, pockets and cuffs separately.
9. Second fitting. Baste skirt to bodice. Pin pockets, collar and sleeves to garment and determine finished sleeve length.
10. Stitch sleeves in armhole and bodice to skirt. Complete pockets.
11. Mark hemline and slip-stitch into place.
12. Sew on buttons, press dress carefully.

Bar Tacks

Worked bar tacks are used to secure the end of a buttonhole or to strengthen the end of an opening. A worked bar is also used on sheer fabrics instead of a metal eye. Strengthen the bar tack by taking the stitches through the back of the fabric. Cover the strands on the outside with a blanket stitch, or wrap the thread tightly around strands (Fig. 4). Heavy thread, like Gütermann Twist, should be used.

Straight tacks are used to reinforce the end of a seam. Take several stitches across the end of the seam or opening, one on top of each other.

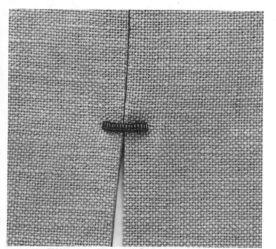
Fig. 4

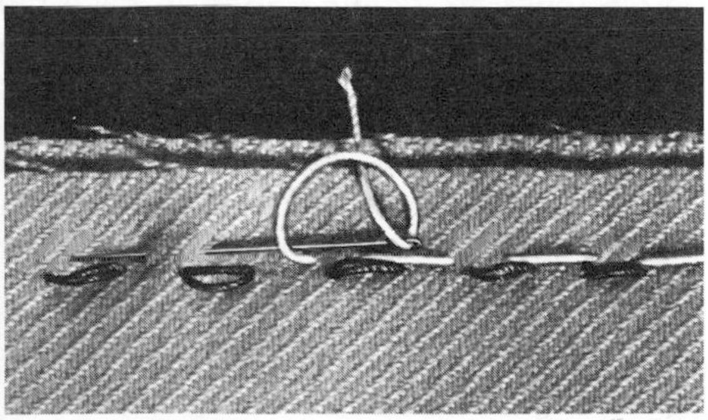

Basting

Basting is used to join two or more pieces of fabric together. For the first fitting, baste together all garment pieces, according to the instructions on the pattern guide. Pin sections right sides together. With basting thread, using small running stitches, baste pieces together. Remove basting thread after seams have been stitched permanently (Fig. 5).

Fig. 5

Machine basting: Use the longest stitch on your machine, the same stitch as you would use for machine gathering. The bobbin thread is easily pulled out, because the tension automatically slackens with this kind of stitch.

The method of holding several pieces of fabric together with DIAGONAL BASTING is explained on page 54.

Basting of a lapped seam with corner: Turn under the edges of the section to be lapped. If fabric is bulky, cut away corner diagonally. Hold cutting edges together with an overhand stitch (Fig. 6). Baste closely along folded edge. Make another row of basting at an even distance of about $\frac{3}{8}''$ (1 cm) underneath. Machine-stitch between the two rows of basting to prevent edges from slipping apart. For a neat finish, machine-stitch close to basting. Remove basting thread afterwards.

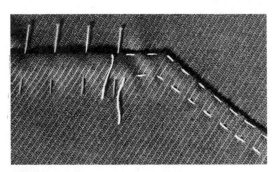

Fig. 6

Beads and Sequins

Beads and sequins come in many colours and shapes. They are used for decorative trimmings on party and evening wear.

Fig. 7

Arrange the sequins with edges overlapping. Sew each sequin to the garment with a tiny back stitch, using Gütermann Sew-all thread. This will anchor each sequin securely, and will prevent the whole row from coming apart in case the thread breaks (Fig. 7). Flat round single sequins may be applied with a bead. Bring the needle through the centre of the sequin and the bead and then back down again through the centre of the sequin and the fabric.

Fig. 8

An ornamental effect is obtained when rod-shaped beads are sewn to the garment at a slant, instead of sewing them next to each other in a straight line (Fig. 8).

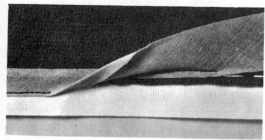

Fig. 9

Fig. 10

Fig. 11

Belting (Bands, Waistline Finishes)

Belting is used for inside skirt bands. Place the seam allowance of the upper skirt edge over the upper edge of the petersham, stitch together with bias binding. Machine or hand-stitch the free edge of the binding with Gütermann Sew-all thread to the petersham (Fig. 9).

Elasticised belting is practical and comfortable. It prevents blouses from slipping out of the skirt, and fits snugly without restricting. Baste the elasticised belting to the right side of the skirt. Stitch to waistline with long or zigzag stitching. Stretch the belting slightly (Fig. 10). The cut edge of the upper skirt edge lies between the skirt and the belting.

A more common method is to finish the waistline of a skirt with a waistband (Fig. 11). Interface the waistband with grossgrain ribbon or petersham. See WAISTBAND page 134 .

Belts

Cut twice the width of the finished belt plus seam allowance. Fold the fabric over the interfacing, overlap at the centre on the inside of the belt. Turn the pointed edge and the end of the belt to the inside. Blind-hem the edges. If preferred, top-stitch along the edges of the belt with Gütermann Sew-all thread, on lighter fabrics. On heavy material use Gütermann Twist (Fig. 12).

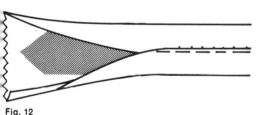

Fig. 12

For a belt with interfacing cut the fabric twice the width of the finished belt. Baste the interfacing with long herring-bone stitches to the wrong side of the back section, with one edge along the centre fold line. Fold the belt in half lengthwise and with right sides together, stitch along the pointed edge and lengthwise edge.

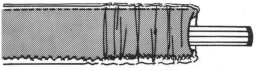

Fig. 13

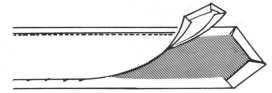

Fig. 14

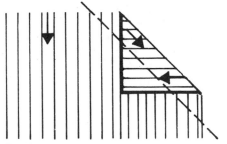

Fig. 15

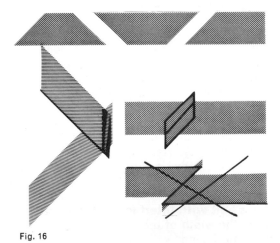

Fig. 16

Trim interfacing close to stitching and turn the belt to the right side.

To turn a belt inside out, insert a pencil inside the turned-in pointed edge (Fig. 13).

Belts faced with leather, grossgrain ribbon or lining: Cut a piece of interfacing the same shape as the belt. Place the fabric over the interfacing or stiffening. Turn all edges of the fabric over the interfacing and baste. Turn under edges of the facing and hand-stitch to the inside of the belt, or top-stitch all along the belt close to edges (Fig. 14).

Bias

Determine bias by folding the cut edge of the fabric at right angles to the selvage. The fold of the fabric shows the true bias (Fig. 15).

Bias Strips

These are fabric strips cut on the bias and joined together with a plain seam on the straight grain of the fabric.

Place one strip on top of the other with right sides together and at right angles. Make a line of stitching parallel to the cut edge. Press the seam open and snip off the projecting ends, thus forming a continuous bias strip with straight edges (Fig. 16). For piping and edging use a bias strip about 1″ (2·5 cm) wide. For heavy and bulky fabrics, finish the raw edges of a seam with a bias strip cut from the lining.

Bias strips attached and embroidered by machine: Insert the self-fabric bias or commercial binding which is available in many colours into the multi-slotted binder attachment of your sewing machine. Bias strips should be 1″ (2·5 cm) wide. This

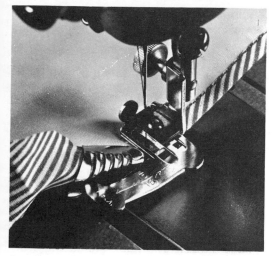

Fig. 17

attachment folds and guides the binding, encasing the cut edges of the fabric in one process. If desired ric-rac braid may be placed between the edges of the bias strip for added decoration (Fig. 17).

Another method is to insert the bias strip in the multi-slotted binder attachment and using one of the embroidery stitches on your machine, attach and embroider the bias strip to the garment in one process (see also Fig. 19).

Bindings and Facings

Fig. 18

Bias facing is used as decoration on the outside of a garment. Facing can be of the same fabric, in a contrasting colour to the garment, or in a completely different fabric.

The bias facing must be pressed into shape, if it is used to finish a curved edge, for example a rounded neckline. This is not necessary if the edge it is to finish is straight (Fig. 18). Stretch the outside edge of the bias facing and ease the bias on the inside edge with an iron. When pressing take care not to crease the facing.

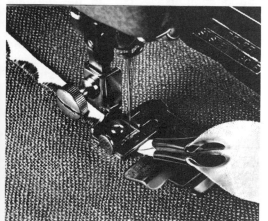

Fig. 19

Narrow bias facing is worked with the multi-slotted binder attachment. Narrow bias facing is obtained by passing the bias strip through the binder. It can now be applied with straight or zigzag stitching either in a straight line, or it can be used for more ornamental designs (Fig. 19).

Gross grain braid can also be pressed into shape under a damp cloth. The braid is pulled into a curved shape by pressing it under a damp cloth.

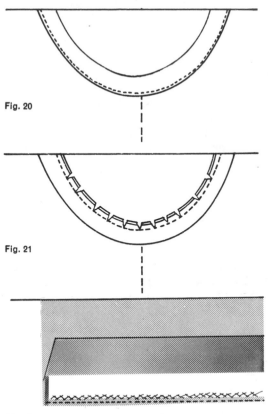

Fig. 20

Fig. 21

Fig. 22

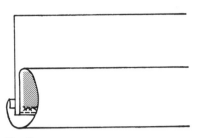

Fig. 23

Shaped facings are cut on the same grain as the edge they are to finish (Fig. 20).

The facing is used to finish the raw edge of a garment: it sometimes overlaps at the lower edge of a sleeve or at the top of a pocket.

Place the right side of the facing to the wrong side of the edge it is to finish. Stitch a plain seam with Gütermann Sew-all thread. Grade seam and clip seam allowance at intervals (Fig. 21). Fold facing to right side. Make a line of basting stitches along the edge of the fold line. Measure even width of the facing from fold edge.

Decorative facings should be clearly visible on the outside of the garment. They are therefore top-stitched from both sides, or slip-stitched by hand to the garment.

If light-weight fabric is used, it is advisable to insert a piece of interfacing underneath the facing. Cut interfacing without seam allowance and fasten with herring-bone stitches to the seamline (Fig. 22). Fold the facing over the interfacing and stitch to inside of the garment. The folding edge is slip-stitched like a cuff to the garment (Fig. 23).

Duchesse facings: Cut the fabric on the bias, fold the fabric strips around a heavy-weight interfacing. Use a padding stitch to hold interfacing to the fabric. Duchesse facings are slip-stitched to the garment.

Blanket Stitch

This simple loop stitch is used for finishing the edges of fabrics. For buttonholes keep stitches close together. Stitches may be more widely spaced when used on

Fig. 24

Fig. 25

Fig. 26

non-fraying edges, or on turned edges. For a decorative finish use a heavy thread such as Gütermann Twist in a contrasting colour (Fig. 24).

The blanket or loop stitch is worked from left to right. Hold fabric edge upwards. Bring needle from the back through the edge of the fabric. Carry the thread over the edge and bring the needle again from the back through the edge. The needle is passed through the loop which has been formed. Draw the thread tight to form a small knot on the upper edge. This type of loop stitch will stay in place.

Bolero

A bolero is a short, open jacket without buttons (Fig. 25). It is worn to complement a dress of the same colour or a contrasting colour. It is cut shorter or longer, depending on fashion.

Bordered Fabrics

Ornamental border designs or embroidery are printed or woven along the lengthwise edge of the fabric. The design serves at the same time as an edge finish. Fabric must be cut on the crosswise grain for a border edge finish (Fig. 26). More fabric than usual is required.

Braids (Foldover and Flat)

Braid is often used to neaten front edges, necklines, collars and pockets.

Baste the facing wrong sides together to front edge. Sandwich interfacing between lining and garment fabric. Baste through all thicknesses. Trim away seam allowance. Stitch the braid with Gütermann Sew-all thread to the outside of the garment. To obtain the desired finished width, place

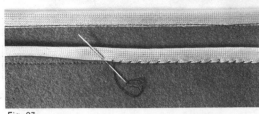
Fig. 27

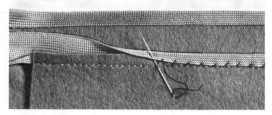
Fig. 28

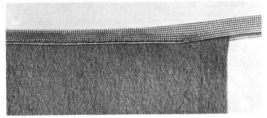
Fig. 29

braid as far back from cutting edge as required. Fold braid over garment edge and hem to inside stitching line (Fig. 27).

For a piped edge effect, stitch the braid to the right side of the garment, then fold braid over the edge of the garment and hem into piace (Fig. 28).

A simple method of applying braid: Fold the braid in half lengthwise. Press the braid, so that one fold is slightly wider than the other. Place the folded braid over fabric edge, with the fold line directly over the edge. Baste well and stitch to garment with the narrow fold on the upper side, taking care to catch the wider underside (Fig. 29).

Lapel edged with braid: When edging lapels, pay special attention to the spot where lapel and front edge are joined. Do not baste braid to garment at this point. Leave braid unattached for about $1\frac{1}{4}''$ (3 cm). The rest of the braid is applied to the front edge, right sides facing, and because the lapel folds to the outside, braid must be basted again after $1\frac{1}{4}''$ (3 cm), right sides together to the edge of the lapel (Fig. 30).

The $1\frac{1}{4}''$ (3 cm) margin is necessary, so the braid lies flat under the presser foot of the machine. Afterwards hand-stitch the un-attached braid section to the garment. Machine-stitch the braid to the outside of the lapel, collar and front edge, then fold over garment edge and hem into place.

The turning of the braid at an inward or outward corner is made easier when the braid is machined flat to the edge of the garment (Fig. 31).

Machine one edge of the braid to the garment. Push the braid slightly together at the point, but draw the braid tight at the inward corner, where collar and lapel meet. Turn the braid to the wrong side of

Fig. 31

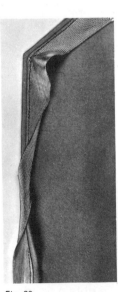
Fig. 30

the garment, make a fold at the point or corner respectively. Fasten the fold of the mitre with a few small stitches.

Ric-rac, corded braid and other trimmings add a personal touch to your garment.

With thread of the same colour as the trimming, stitch close along both edges, or apply by machine with a zigzag stitch.

Ric-rac braid is applied with a straight line of stitching through the centre. If used as an edging, stitch the ric-rac over the edge of the garment, so that one side of the pointed edge overlaps. (See page 103 for more information.)

Corded braid is applied with a straight line of stitching between the scallops as shown on our example (Fig. 32). (See page 25.)

Fig. 32

Very ornamental braid should be applied by hand. A narrow woollen braid or a fringe can be applied flat to the garment with a zigzag stitch.

Finish raw edges of fabric before applying any kind of trimmings.

Buckles

Buckles covered with the same material as the dress complete the overall effect of a garment.

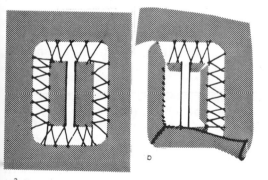

a

b

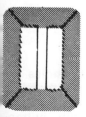

c

Fig. 33

Place the buckle form on the wrong side of a piece of fabric. Attach with over-lapping herring-bone stitches to the fabric (a). Stitches must not show on the right side of the fabric. Trim the edges of the fabric piece to one and a half times the width of the buckle you wish to cover. Cut open fabric between the buckle and the buckle bar. Place the inside fabric edges over the buckle, fold the outside edges over it. Make a fold at each corner of the buckle and oversew with an overhand stitch (*b*). The seam should be on the wrong side of the buckle. The centre bar remains uncovered and should later be completely concealed by the belt (Fig. 33 *a*, *b* and *c*).

Burr or Nylon Hook Tape Fastener, e.g. Velcro

This fastener consists of two tapes (made from synthetic fibres). Tiny hooks are attached to one side of the tape and fleece to the other. The hooks will cling firmly to the tiny loops on the soft side of the tape. Sew tape to the overlap and underlap of an opening. Even under light pressure the two sides of the tape will stick to each other and keep the garment securely fastened. For easy opening just separate edges with a pull (Fig. 34).

Fig. 34

Bust Measurement

For adult clothing select pattern size according to bust measurement. The method used to take measurements is explained on page 68.

The three sketches (Fig. 35) show how profiles can differ, even when they have the same bust measurements. It is of importance to compare the remaining measurements given on the pattern with your own, and to adjust the pattern accordingly before cutting. See PATTERN ADJUSTMENT page 85.

Button Closing

Garment edges in which buttonholes are to be made should be firm. It is therefore advisable to sew seam binding to the wrong side of the fabric under the buttonhole location line. Or baste interfacing to

Fig. 35

the inside of garment, wide enough to extend at least 1″ to 1¼″ (2·5 cm to 3 cm) over the buttonhole marking.

Buttonholes

Buttonholes are worked on the right side of the garment for women and on the left side for men.

Hand-worked buttonholes are made after the garment is completed. Bound buttonholes are made through the garment before the facing is applied.

How to mark a horizontal buttonhole: The distance between the end of the buttonhole marking, which should extend about $\frac{1}{10}$″ (2 mm) over the centre front marking, and the edge of garment, should be about the same length as the button itself. The button should be placed at the centre of the garment with the edge of the closing extending half the length of the button (Fig. 36).

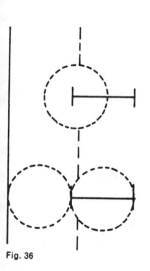

Fig. 36

Plain hand-made buttonholes: The buttonhole is worked with Gütermann Sew-all thread, for lighter garments. With heavy fabrics, use Gütermann Twist. Cut buttonhole through double thickness of fabric. Oversew cut edges of buttonhole. Use a close buttonhole stitch and with cut edge upwards work from right to left, or from left to right. The thread is carried under the needle (Fig. 37).

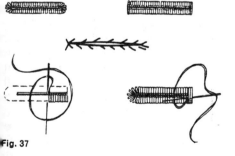

Fig. 37

Vertical worked buttonholes for front closings are finished at both ends with bar tacks, or make a bar tack at one end and secure the other end where the button is located with ray-shaped stitches (Fig. 37).

Fig. 38

Tailored hand-made buttonholes are used in heavy fabric. Cut a circular hole at one end of the buttonhole and using a blanket stitch make ray-shaped stitches

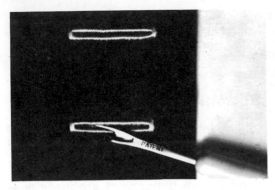

Fig. 39

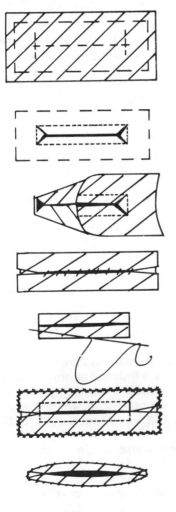

Fig. 40

around the hole. Work blanket stitch over fine cord or bead yarn (Fig. 38) and finish the other end with a small bar tack.

Machine-made buttonholes: Make a row of closely spaced zigzag stitching around basting line. For a stronger buttonhole carry a thread along under zigzag stitching. Bar tacks on each end are also worked with several zigzag stitches. Cut the buttonhole very carefully between the stitching with buttonhole cutter (Fig. 39).

Bound buttonholes: Length of buttonhole markings must show on both sides of fabric (Fig. 40).
Cut oblong piece of fabric for binding on bias and press lengthwise under damp cloth. Pin and tack to right side of garment over markings. Using Gütermann Sew-all thread, stitch outline with small stitches on wrong side of garment: stitch $\frac{1}{8}''$ (2–3 mm) from marking line, along each side and across both ends, overlapping stitches to fasten ends of thread.
Cut buttonhole through centre to within $\frac{3}{8}''$ (4 mm) of each end and then diagonally into each corner, taking care not to cut into machine stitches.
Pull fabric piece for binding through opening and press seam allowances downwards and away from buttonhole.
Roll binding fabric into neat piping on both buttonhole edges, forming small inverted pleats at ends on underside. Tack piping edges lightly together and secure with small handsewing stitches through stitching line fold on outside.
Herringbone fabric pieces to inside of garment and press.
To open buttonhole through facing fabric covering fastening, make cut slightly longer than buttonhole. Turn under cut edges and hem to buttonhole fabric.

Piped buttonholes are worked by using a piece of fabric, leather or braid in a contrasting colour, which is folded lengthwise. Open out and fold both edges to

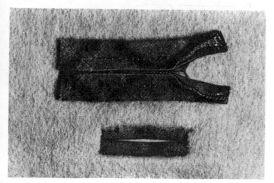

Fig. 41

centre marking. Baste the strip over buttonhole marking on the right side of the garment. Stitch along each side and across both ends the required length of the buttonhole. The outside facing must be half as wide as the finished buttonhole. Cut buttonhole through centre marking. Clip diagonally to corners. Turn facing to inside. The folded edges will meet at the centre of the opening, forming an even binding along each side of the buttonhole. Push the triangular ends to inside and slip-stitch, or secure with bar tacks (Fig. 41).

Buttons

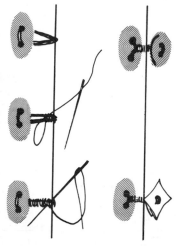

Fig. 42

Buttons serve as a decoration and fastening on a garment. They are always sewn to the garment with strong thread and to double thickness of fabric. (For light fabrics, use Gütermann Sew-all thread; for heavy material use Gütermann Twist.) If this is not possible, place a piece of fabric for reinforcement to underside of garment or sew a smaller button beneath it on the inside. For easier buttoning, flat buttons are sewn to the garment with a thread shank. Hold button slightly away from fabric, this will allow for longer stitches to be made. Wind thread tightly around stitches, forming stem. Fasten thread securely (Fig. 42). Buttons can also be sewn to garment with machine zigzag stitches: this saves time, especially for shirts, etc. (Fig. 43).

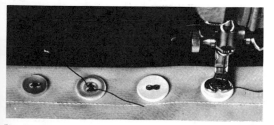

Fig. 43

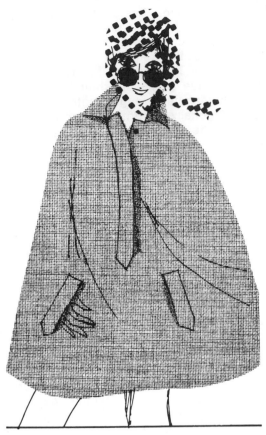

Fig. 44

Fig. 45

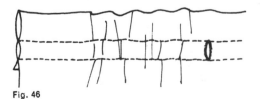

Fig. 46

Cape

A cape is a sleeveless cloak and some-times has a fly front closure. It is very popular with both sexes for protection against all kinds of weather.

The design shown in the illustration (Fig. 44) is made from coarse woollen material or unmilled woollen cloth. The fly front makes it especially windproof.

Casing

A casing is a hem with an opening, so that elastic can be inserted..Turn under edge of fabric, the width of the elastic plus $\frac{5}{8}''$ (1·5 cm) seam allowance. Turn raw edge under about $\frac{1}{8}''$ (3 mm) and stitch into place close to the edge. Edge-stitch along upper fold line, close to the edge, or make a false hem of the required width (Fig. 45).

Casing with heading: Work in the same way as above but make the hem wider, to obtain the required width for the heading. Make two rows of stitching for the casing. Insert elastic or ribbon. The gathered heading will be above the casing. Make a small opening in the casing, so that the elastic or ribbon can be drawn through. Finish the opening with buttonhole stitches (Fig. 46).

Faced casing: Cut a strip of fabric (the width of the elastic plus seam allowance). Turn under seam allowance on both sides of the facing. Stitch the lengthwise sides with Gütermann Sew-all thread to the fabric. Keep stitching close to edges. It is advisable to make the opening for the ribbon or elastic in the seam, or if the casing is a short one, machine the elastic to the side of the casing (Fig. 47).

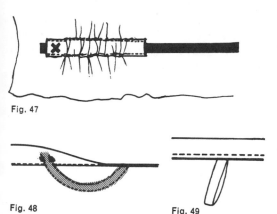

Fig. 47

Fig. 48

Fig. 49

Coat Tabs

Coat tabs are loops made from firm lining. To strengthen tab, insert a piece of cording. The fabric loop is pressed flat and into a slightly curved shape. Sew with a double thread of Gütermann Sew-all thread to collar seam line and hem the lining over it (Fig. 48). On skirts, place the fabric loop between the waistband before stitching waistband to the skirt (Fig. 49).

Collars

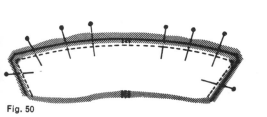

Fig. 50

Collars should be finished separately, before they are attached to the neck edge of a garment. Collars made from sheer fabrics are interfaced to prevent seams from showing through. To interface a collar, pin the upper and the under collar right sides together and baste the interfacing over the upper collar section (Fig. 50).

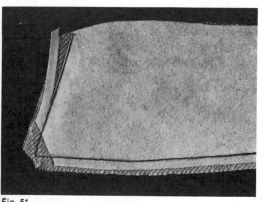

Fig. 51

Top and undercollar: For a flat finish, cut the undercollar on the bias. The upper and under collar sections are stitched together on three sides. To keep edges flat and to avoid bulk at corners, the corners are cut off $\frac{1}{4}''$ (6 mm) diagonally on the outside edge of the interfacing. After stitching the seams, trim interfacing close to stitching and grade seam allowance of collar (Fig. 51). It is not necessary to cut off corners of collars made from sheer fabrics, just fold in corners when turning collar to the right side.

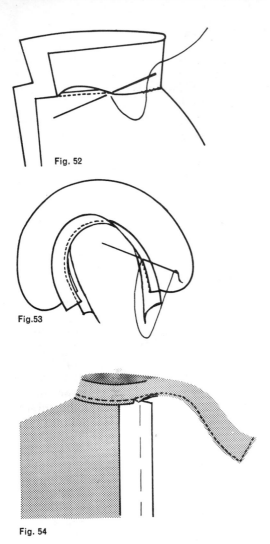

Fig. 52

Fig.53

Fig. 54

Shirtwaist collar is stitched with the top collar section to neck edge if worn open, the undercollar section is slip-stitched to the inner neck seam line (Fig. 52).

For collars which are worn closed at the neck, reverse the process: the undercollar is stitched to the neck edge and the upper collar section is slip-stitched to the inner seam line.

Round curved collars are attached to the neckline with bias facing. Baste the finished collar and the bias strip to the right side of the garment neck edge. Stitch collar and bias facing together using Gütermann Sew-all thread. Fold the free edge of the bias strip over seam allowance and slip-stitch to inside of the collar (Fig. 53).

Tie Collar: Cut two straight strips of fabric. The length depends upon whether you want to tie a bow tie or a short knot. Stitch strips together to make one long strip, then fold it in half lengthwise with right sides together and baste with the upper side to the neck edge, matching joining seam to centre back. Stitch along the neck edge up to $\frac{1}{4}''$ (6 mm) before the centre opening, clip seam allowance here and continue to stitch tie ends. Turn collar right sides out. Turn under seam allowance and slip-stitch to inside over neck seam line. Fold the overlapping edges of the front closing against each other and slip-stitch (Fig. 54).

Shirt collars consist of a collar and a collar band. Cut collar band twice. After turning collar to the right side, stitch one section of the collar band to each side of the collar with right sides together. Turn collar band down. Stitch the inner section of the collar band to inside of shirt with Gütermann Sew-all thread. Stitch the free edge of the collar band over the seam on

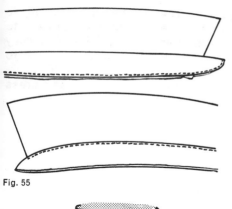

Fig. 55

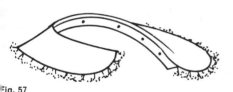

Fig. 56

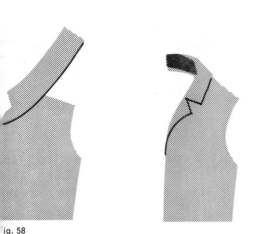

Fig. 57

the right side of the garment. Top-stitch over edge of band (Fig. 55).

Stand-up or mandarin collar: This type of collar should never stand up straight from the neck edge, it should adapt itself to the shape of the neck (Fig. 56). The stand-up or mandarin collar needs a stiff interfacing. Attach the interfacing to the wrong side of collar. Stitch collar seams and clip curved seam allowance, turn collar to the right side. The seam should lie in the fold line, or top-stitch close to the folding edge. Stitch collar to neck opening, with right sides together. Trim away interfacing and slip-stitch inner edge of collar to neckline seam.

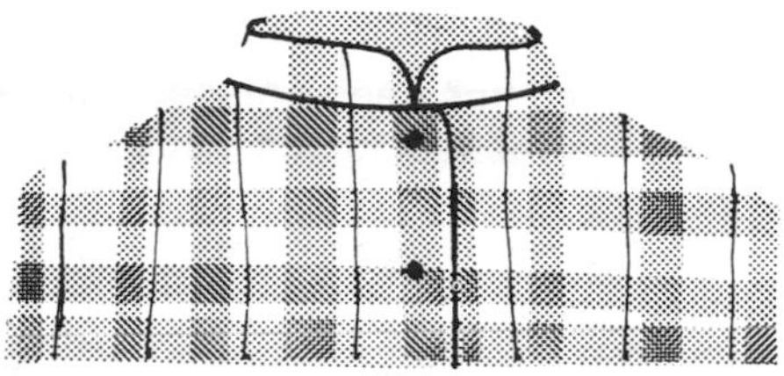

Detachable collars, cuffs or edgings are worked separately. Attach to the finished garment with basting stitches, small buttons or press studs. Removable edgings can also be attached with nylon burr tape (Velcro) to the inside neck or lower sleeve edge (Fig. 57). The latter is convenient for children's dresses.

Revers and shawl collar: For plain shaped shawl or curved collars, attach the undercollar separately to the neck opening. The facing is cut in one. Stitch the undercollar to the neck edge, press seam open. Clip the seam allowance at several intervals at the curve of the neck, so that seam allowance lies flat. The facing is placed over it (Fig. 58).

Watch out for the point where the neck and shoulder seams meet. The revers facing should be notched at this point, to ensure a flat finish. The facing is slip-stitched to the inside of the neck line and secured with a few stitches at the inner shoulder seam.

Fig. 58

Fig. 59

Collar with revers: Stitch the facing to the two front edges of the garment to where collar joins the neckline. Cut away seam allowance from line of stitching to the point where the collar joins the neckline. Turn the facing to inside and press well (Fig. 59).

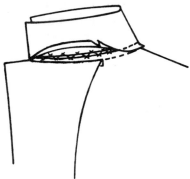

Fig. 60

The collar, which has been finished separately, is now attached to the neck opening. The right side of the undercollar is stitched to the right side of the coat neck edge. Press seam open. Fasten the seam allowance of the undercollar with herringbone stitches to the interfacing. Clip the neck edge seam allowance at intervals to ensure it lies flat. Clip the seam allowance of the upper collar at the shoulder seam point. With back stitches attach the upper collar to the neck seam line, along the whole length of neck opening (Fig. 60).

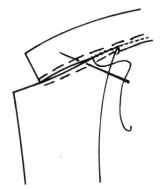

Fig. 61

The edges of the upper collar and the facing (as far as the shoulder seam) are turned under, and with the two folded edges touching each other are sewn together by hand (Fig. 61).

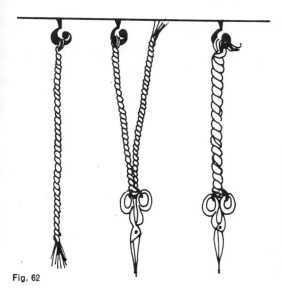

Fig. 62

Cord, twisted

A hand-worked cord (Fig. 62) has the advantage that it can be made in any colour and size according to one's own requirements.

Cut several strands of Gütermann Twist. Each strand should be five times the finished length of the cord. Attach the strands to a hook and twist in one direction until they are fairly tight. Now fold the cord in half, thread through the handles of a pair of scissors and attach the other end to the hook. The weight of the scissors will twist the free hanging strands to a firm cord of their own accord.

Fig. 63

Corded Braid

Braid and ribbons with a raised effect can be used as trimmings on dresses and home furnishings. Stitching should be as inconspicuous as possible and fine thread like Gütermann Sew-all thread should be used. Attach with an overhand stitch, using matching thread and keeping stitches inside the loop holes (Fig. 63).

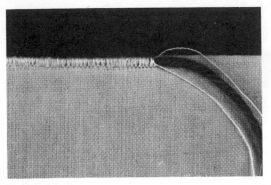

Fig. 64

Fig. 65

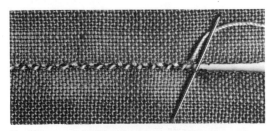

Fig. 66

Corded Edging

With a close machine zigzag stitch oversew thick threads or narrow ribbons, which are passed through a binder attachment (Fig. 64).

Corsage (Boned Underbodice)

A corsage is a bodice stiffened with metal or bone strips, which are shaped to your figure. It is worn under a strapless dress, to give it a perfect fit.

A built-in bra is indispensable for a figure with a large bust *(Fig. 65)*.

Cross Seam Stitch

Straight selvage edges of fabrics, lace and ribbons can be joined with this firm and nearly invisible stitch, i.e. patching. With needle pick up a few threads from each fabric edge, pull stitches tightly. This method of joining gives a specially flat finished seam, as there are no turned under edges (Fig. 66).

Cuffs

Sewn-on cuffs: Turn upper and under cuff section over interfacing to right side. Stitch right side of cuff section and interfacing to wrong side of sleeve edge, matching seams. Trim seam allowance of interfacing. Press seam allowances towards cuff. Turn under edge of under cuff section and hem to seam line.

Or: Place the completed cuff over the outside of lower edge of sleeve. Place bias strip over the edges and stitch them together, press seam allowance and bias strip towards sleeve and hem-stitch bias strip over seam allowance (Fig. 67).

Fig. 67

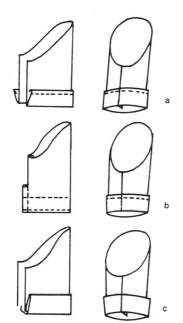

Fig. 68

Cuffs cut-in-one with sleeve (Fig. 68 a–c): Before stitching underarm seam of sleeve, turn under lower edge of sleeve. Turn up cuff hem and edge-stitch to sleeve. Use a French seam to stitch underarm seam together. A plain seam will not give a neat enough appearance on the inside of sleeve (Fig. 68 a).

Stitch underarm seam from the top to the inside of cuff. Turn sleeve to right side and stitch seam to the lower edge. Turn up cuff and edge-stitch or slip-stitch to sleeve (Fig. 68 b).

Cut the cuff two and a half times the width of the required cuff when finished, turn to inside along fold line. Turn and stitch a narrow fold at the inside. Turn up cuff. Stitch underarm with a French seam (Fig. 68 c).

Cuffs for shirt blouses: Shirt cuffs must have a bound opening at sleeve edge (see page 78).

Stitch and turn upper and under section of cuff over interfacing to right side. Stitch under section of cuff to inside of lower edge of sleeve. Distribute fullness towards placket opening. Turn under free edge of cuff and top-stitch over seam on right side. Make buttonhole (Fig. 69).

For more elegant blouses, stitch right side of cuff to right side of sleeve, fold cuff and slip-stitch to inside of sleeve.

The French cuff is made in a similar way as shirt cuff. Apply cuff, top-stitch over seam on right side and continue top-stitching around the entire cuff. Be careful when marking buttonholes, because the folded cuff should cover seamline of cuff and sleeve edge. Make machine or hand-worked buttonholes.

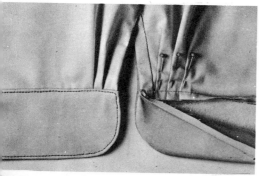

Fig. 69

Cutting

Fabrics up to 36″ (90 cm) wide are known as single-width fabrics; fabrics between 40″ and 60″ (100 and 150 cm) wide are known as double-width fabrics. The lengthwise grain or 'warp' runs parallel to the selvage, the crosswise grain or 'weft' from selvage to selvage. The grain line arrow on each pattern piece indicates the warp or straight grain of the fabric. Place pattern pieces with ends of arrows at an even distance from selvage or straight thread. This should on no account be altered as it might unfavourably affect the appearance, fit and hang of the garment. Only after examining the structure of the fabric carefully, and in exceptional circumstances may the grain line arrows be placed parallel to the crosswise grain. In this case the pattern pieces for the whole of the garment must be placed in this manner. This is sometimes necessary when the width of the cloth is narrow and the bodice is to be cut in one with the sleeves on the crosswise fold line, without a back or front seam.

The layouts shown here use the same pattern but different fabrics (Figs. 70 a, b, c and d). For a better comparison, the fabric used in all layouts is 36″ (90 cm) wide, and the pattern is placed on single thickness of fabric only. Facings, bias strips, collar sections and belts are included in the yardage, but for the sake of lucidity not shown in the layout. For practical reasons it is better to place the inner cutting edge of facings exactly along the selvage, i.e. the firmly woven edge of the fabric.

Fig. 70 a: Materials that are non-woven or knitted like felt or Vilene have neither a right nor wrong side, nor do they have a grain line. They hang properly and drape well cut in any direction. Therefore pattern pieces can be placed on the fabric in the most economical manner.

Fig. 70 a

Fig. 70 b

Fig. 70 b: Fabrics with nap or tiny one-way designs. Among the most important are shiny silk fabrics, velours and velvets. When using shiny velvet for a dress, the pile should run downwards. For a richer colour, cut dull velvet against the nap, with the pile running upwards. All pattern pieces must be placed in the same direction.

Fig. 70 c: Fabrics without nap or irregular prints can be cut in two directions. This means that pattern pieces can be placed in opposite directions in order to save material.

Fig. 70 d: More material is needed when using fabrics with large one-way designs or border prints. For a pleasing overall effect, try matching the design when cutting collar and facings. Stripes and checks, especially when they are uneven, need special care to match the design. Place all pattern pieces symmetrically on the fabric. This of course requires more material. In this case make a centre seam at the back of the garment, so that the design is identical on both sides (Fig. 71).

Diagonal and ribbed fabrics should be matched to form an angle at straight seams. This can be done when one skirt section is placed lengthwise on the fabric and the second section is placed crosswise.

Crosswise grain line arrows on pattern pieces should be given special attention when placing on the fabric.

When the same pattern piece is used for the left and the right side, reverse the pattern piece for the second section, otherwise you will end up with two identical sections (Fig. 72).

Fig. 70 c   Fig. 70 d

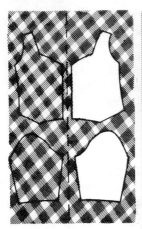

Fig. 72

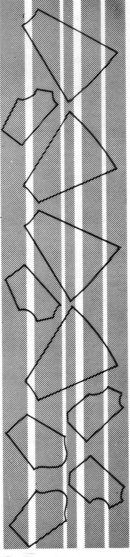

Fig. 71

Cutting rules

1. Straighten ends of fabric, pull a cross-wise thread and cut across fabric width. Or clip one selvage and tear fabric with caution.

2. Fold fabric in half lengthwise, right sides facing.

3. Pin pattern pieces to fabric as shown in the layout or according to the diagram. Pattern pieces without a centre seam, are placed on the fold of the fabric.

4. Allow enough seam allowance, about $\frac{3}{4}''$ (2 cm) for necklines, $1\frac{1}{4}''$ (3 cm) for waistline seams, and $2''$ (5 cm) for hems. Allow more for children's dresses.

5. Check grain line. Do not forget to reverse pattern pieces that are cut on single thickness of fabric only. Check that no pieces have been forgotten.

6. Cut out garment and tailor tack all markings necessary for assembly.

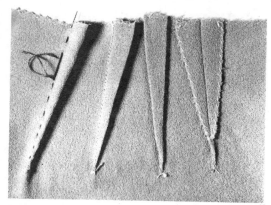
Fig. 73

Darts

Darts are stitched folds tapered to a point. They are used to assist in moulding the garment. Baste dart from point to wide end, but stitch the dart with Gütermann Sew-all thread from wide end to point (Figs. 73 and 75). On heavy fabric slash through centre of dart and press open (Fig. 74). Darts in light fabrics should be pressed to one side. The width of the dart may vary according to the contours of your individual figure. Adjustments may be necessary when fitting the garment.

Double-pointed darts in one-piece dresses fit better, if dart is clipped close to the centre stitching.

Darts are generally pressed flat towards centre of garment.

The seam is especially inconspicuous, when dart is pressed box pleated with fold over stitching.

Fig. 74

Darts, the construction of

The point of each dart should point towards the fullest part of the body, or the widest part of a dart tuck must be released towards the fullest part of the body (Fig. 76).

(a) Bust dart: Stitch with the front edge on the straight grain of the fabric and pointing vertically towards the bust. It is important that the last two or three stitches at the point of the dart are taken directly on the fold in order to avoid tucks. Darts should be pressed towards the centre of the garment.

(b) Slanted underarm dart: This dart allows more material to be used and is therefore especially suitable for the fuller figure. Press downwards.

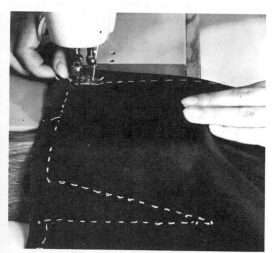
Fig. 75

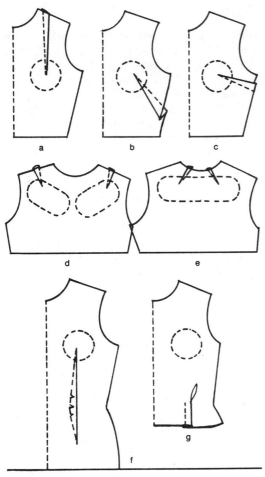

Fig. 76

(c) Horizontal dart: This dart runs crosswise to the side seam and ends short of the fullest part of the bust. The dart is short and narrow. Use this dart for small busts. Horizontal darts are especially inconspicuous and nearly invisible on garments made from patterned fabric. Press flat downwards.

(d) Shoulder dart: Shoulder darts are only needed when shoulder blades protrude. They must not be too long and are hardly visible when ironed out flat.

(e) Neckline dart: Neckline darts are necessary for full necks. Small darts are stitched ray-shaped starting from neck edge. Press towards the centre of the garment.

(f) Double-pointed dart: The dart runs parallel to the centre of the body. Close fitting dresses fit better if the dart is clipped close to the centre stitching.

(g) Dart tuck: This dart is used to give shaping to blouses from the lower edge to the waist. The dart releases its fullness in an unpressed tuck towards the bust. Press the stitched part of the dart towards the centre of the garment. It prevents the blouse slipping out of waistband of skirt.

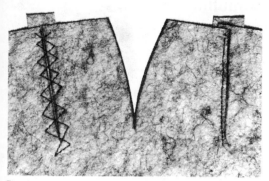

Fig. 77

Dart in Underlining and Interfacing

In order to avoid bulk, the dart is cut out when using non-woven underlining or interfacing which does not fray at the raw edge. Baste edge where they touch one another. Place a strip of fabric underneath and straight stitch in zigzag lines or zigzag stitching over it.

Narrow darts are slashed along the centre marking. Overlap the edges of the slash, place a strip of fabric underneath and sew the two sections together (Fig. 77).

Decorative Stitching

See TOP STITCHING (page130).

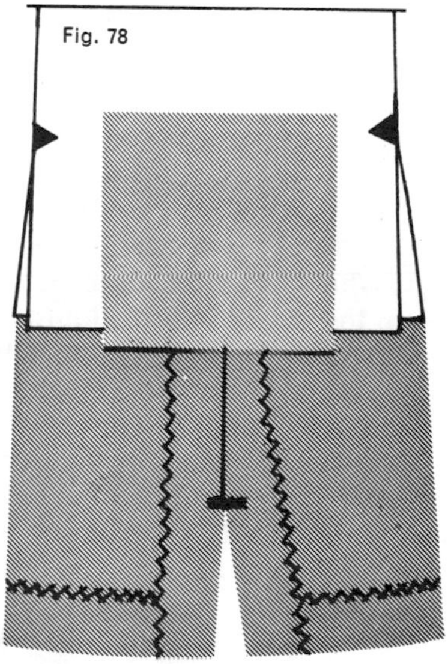

Fig. 78

Dior Slit

Sometimes called a Dior pleat, it is a slit at the centre back of the skirt or dress. It opens over the skirt lining, which has a wide hem edging made from the same material as the skirt. This kind of slit gives ample freedom of movement. The centre back seam is cut with a wide seam allowance. The lining is cut according to the pattern. For the slit opening, leave centre back seam open for about 6" (15 cm). Finish raw edges of seam allowance and slip-stitch to the inside of the skirt. The turned-up hem is placed under the seam allowance of the slit opening (Fig. 79). Secure the top of the opening with a bar tack, or stitch a triangle of the lining to it (Fig. 78).

Fig. 79

Place lining inside skirt and baste to waistline. Sew lining into waistband.

For easier ironing, lining is not sewn to side seams of skirt, but left hanging loose.

Doubling (Facing)

Doubling means sewing two pieces of fabric together.

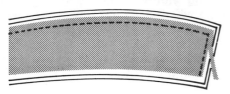
Fig. 80

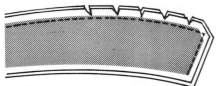
Fig. 81

Collars, pockets or cuffs are cut twice. Baste the two sections right sides together and machine-stitch with Gütermann Sew-all thread.

Collars and cuffs are often interfaced. Trim the interfacing close to the seamline (Fig. 80). Grade the seam allowance of collar or cuffs. Cut away seam allowance close to stitching at curved edges or cut diagonally across points. For inside curves clip seam allowance for outside notch (Fig. 81). Do not cut away the points if you use a light-weight fabric, but fold in seam allowance before turning the two sections to the right side.

Turn the two fabric pieces so that the seam lies between the two sections. Baste round the outer edges and press lightly. Remove basting thread and press again under a damp cloth.

Draping

A design which requires draping is very suitable for the larger figure. Figure irregularities can often be corrected with the skilful draping of fabrics. Drapes need constant fittings to achieve the desired result. The rather soft effect of draping gives a more elegant appearance to any garment (Fig. 82). Always choose a soft, drapable fabric.

Transfer the pattern markings, which determine the exact location of the drapes to the fabric, and they should be gathered or pleated accordingly. Careful consideration should be given to the grain line of the fabric and the location of the folds, as both are essential for a well-draped dress.

Fig. 82

For a better fit, small weights are sometimes inserted into the drapes. Sometimes a slight stretching of the folds will suffice.

Dress Shields

Dress shields are made from two layers of fabric with a water-repellent or rubber interlining. Dress shields protect your garment from perspiration and should be tacked inside the garment.

Duffle Coat

This is a knee-length, short sports coat, practical for men and women alike. Typical for this type of coat made from impregnated poplin or woollen material are toggle fastenings and a low joined yoke. If the coat is reversible, it can be worn depending on the weather with the wool lining on the outside (Fig. 83).

Fig. 83

Ease Allowance

Ease allowance is necessary for the comfortable fit of a garment, especially for suits and coats. This ease allowance is provided in every pattern.

Easing Fullness

Follow the instructions as indicated on your pattern. Place a line of small running stitches along the section which is to be eased, or use a machine basting stitch. Gently draw up the lower thread to adjust the fullness. Place the section over a tailor's ham or a rolled-up towel and proceed to shrink out the fullness under a damp cloth with an iron (Fig. 84).

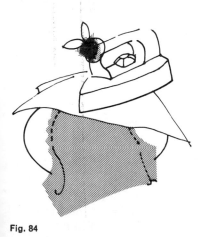

Fig. 84

Edge-to-Edge Seam

Cutting edges that do not fray are held together with this type of seam, for instance when patching. Oversew the two edges by using a zigzag stitch. Keep both edges flat (Fig. 85 top). This is a most satisfactory method when joining torn sheets.

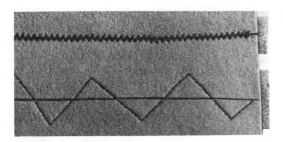

Fig. 85

Seams that do not show on the surface can also be joined with a zigzag stitch. Place a thin strip of lining material underneath the seam for reinforcement (Fig. 85 bottom).

If you have a machine that will straight-stitch only, bring both edges close together, place a strip of lining material beneath and machine into place in zigzag fashion (Fig. 86). Hand-stitched edge-to-edge seams hardly show in heavy fabrics. They are ideal when used for joining small seams, that do not suffer heavy wear.

Fig. 86

Use the darning method for very heavy materials. Join the two pieces of material by using a darning stitch. Insert needle in the edge of the fabric and bring out $\frac{1}{8}''$ (3 mm) from edge, re-insert needle again into the thickness of the second edge. Pull thread tight, bringing both edges close together. Use a matching coloured fine thread of Gütermann Sew-all thread, or a long thread from the fabric itself. Finally raise the nap carefully and hold over steam (Fig. 87).

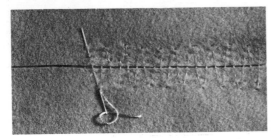

Fig. 87

Edging

The raw edges of necklines, armholes and sleeves can be finished with bias binding or shaped facings.

Pockets, collars and necklines are often edged with a fine rayon braid or soutache braid. Press the bias band into the required shape before applying to garment.

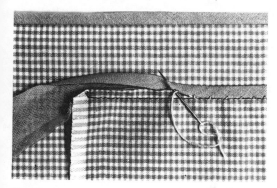

Fig. 88

Shaped or bias bands are stitched with Gütermann Sew-all thread, right sides together to the garment. The binding is pressed over the seam allowance and then folded over the raw edge of the garment. Turn under the raw edge of the binding and slip-stitch to the seamline (Fig. 88). Take care not to stretch the curved section of the garment when applying bias binding.

Embroidery Transfer

Iron on with a hot iron to fabric. Embroider by hand or machine. It is advisable to test heat effect on a scrap of fabric before starting (Fig. 89).

Fig. 89

Eyelets

Mark a circle and make running stitches around the mark. Make a crosswise incision within the line of marking, turn down the corners to the wrong side and work over the edge with blanket stitches, keeping stitches close together. Trim the projecting fabric next to the blanket stitch and shape the eyelet with a bodkin (Fig. 90). Use Gütermann Sew-all thread on fine fabrics, Gütermann Twist on heavy materials.

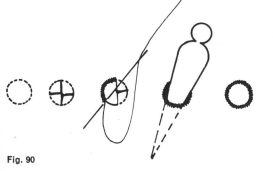

Fig. 90

Fabric Finishes

The textile industry improves the appearance and serviceability of fabric through special treatments. Fabrics can be made water-repellent, crease-resistant, flame-proof or can be given a shrink-resistant finish by a special chemical process. These finishes will be retained after washing and ironing, unlike finishes which are not wash-fast and have to be renewed by starching. The textile industry provides small instruction labels with symbols.

From these symbols you can see whether to wash your fabric in lukewarm or hot water, the temperature control setting for ironing and the most suitable kind of dry cleaning. If you take note of these symbols, damage to your fabric can be prevented. (See page 61.)

100% synthetic fabrics, e.g. **Nylon** and **Polyester,** should only be pressed with an iron which has a temperature control. Press seams and hems under a slightly damp cloth.

Nowadays many fabrics are already sanforized. Woollen materials are steampressed by machine which prevents shrinkage. Other materials are given a crease-resistant finish with synthetic resin. Press this type of material with a cool iron (rayon temperature).

Blended fabrics made from wool and synthetics require a low temperature control setting, otherwise you may damage the fabric. Synthetic fibres will melt if pressed with a too hot iron. For these reasons seams and hems should always be pressed with an iron which has a temperature control. For blended fabrics use the setting which is suitable for the predominant fabric used in the blend. Always place a damp cloth over the fabric before you begin to press.

See page 76 for Thread Chart.

Fabric Tubing

Fabric tubing is made from a cut strip of bias fabric. These are used for loops, binding and piping. With right sides together fold lengthwise a true bias strip 1″ to 1¼″ (2·5 to 3 cm) wide. Stitch ¼″ (5 mm) from fold with Gütermann Sew-all thread. Stretch strip slightly while sewing, otherwise the thread will break when turning the tube inside out.

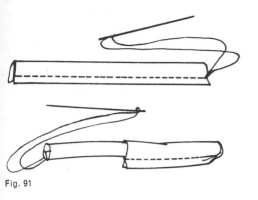

Fig. 91

Fig. 92

Do not trim seam allowance. The seam allowance forms the filler for the tubing, but trim seam allowance if a flat tubing is desired. Attach a strong thread to the end of tube at the seam. Draw the thread through the tubing with a bodkin. Continue pulling end of tube through tubing to turn to right side (Fig. 91).

This method is not suitable for heavy fabrics. For heavy fabrics take the bias strip, turn both raw edges to the inside and close with a slip-stitch (Fig. 92).

Facings for Front Closings

Facings for front closings are either cut in one with the garment (Fig. 93 a), or they are cut separately. For a neater edge, apply interfacing before folding facing to the inside of the garment. The interfacing has to be cut wide enough to reach to the shoulder seam, as this will prevent the rolling of the interfacing edges when facing is folded to the inside of the garment. Interfacing can also be stitched to fold line of cut-in-one facings. This method is especially suitable for children's and washable dresses (Fig. 93 b). Interfacing can also be attached with herringbone stitches, if the garment is made from a loosely woven fabric (Fig. 93 c).

If the facing is applied separately, baste the interfacing to inside of bodice section. Stitch facing to bodice right sides together and on the seam line indicated by your pattern. Trim seam allowance of interfacing close to seam line (Fig. 93 d).

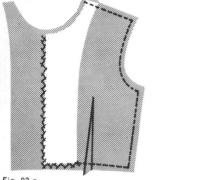

Fig. 93 a

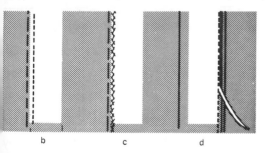

b   c   d

Faggoting

Faggoting is used to join two finished fabric edges with an open worked stitch.

Baste two fabric sections about ½″ (1 cm)

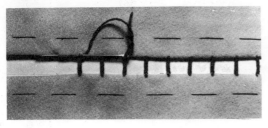

Fig. 94

apart, to a piece of cardboard. Carry the thread through the fold to the opposite edge. Bring the needle back, wrapping thread several times round the bar, insert the needle again into the hold of the first stitch. Continue in this manner.

This type of hemstitch has the advantage that it can be used regardless of the grain line of the fabric (Fig. 94).

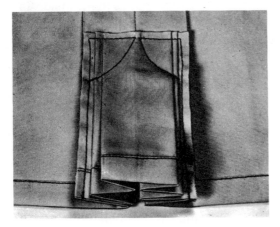

Fig. 95

Fan Pleated Underlay

Work in the same way as for the inverted pleat underlay. Fan pleating consists of several pleats, with the folded edges lying exactly over one another, but on the back of the pleat they should overlap slightly, so that the depth of the pleats decreases. To keep the pleats in a flat position, attach the upper edge with herring-bone stitches to the skirt seam allowance. Make a curved seam as shown in the illustration and secure the pleats with bar tacks (Fig. 95).

Fashion Hints

You and your garment should harmonise if you want to be considered well-dressed. A well-tailored dress may look perfect, but may not necessarily suit your type, and this is what you really want to aim for.

Try to analyse yourself. Find out what your figure type requires, what your best features are and if there are any figure imperfections that you wish to camouflage.

It is not enough to define your type by establishing whether you are tall or short, slim or just the opposite. Your mirror must tell you whether you are slender or 'compact'. Study yourself, and decide whether bright or more subdued colours are more flattering to your skin and hair. Age and personality should also be taken into account, as they also decide colour, fabric as well as the design of your garment. All these facets should be carefully considered, only then will you find your true figure type.

Before you decide on a pattern, stand in front of the mirror and hold the material against you. Fabric design and the fabric's drapability should be taken into consideration in your choice of pattern. The appearance of your garment will improve if attention is given to these factors.

Try to make the workmanship of your garment faultless, as this will give your clothes the professional look, which will be the envy of your friends.

Study the instructions given in this book carefully and it will help you to make your task easier.

If you have a **plump figure** avoid strong colours, shiny fabrics, wide vertical and horizontal stripes, large checks or prints, wide skirts and large collars. More flattering are fine textured and soft fabrics in subdued colours, delicate stripes or tiny prints.

If you are a courageous type wear what you like, but be prepared for criticism (Fig. 96).

Short and slender women may choose lively colours and prints and a more sophisticated style. Choose dresses, suits and coats that accentuate the waist. Slightly flared skirts and narrow sleeves are figure flattering.

Large checks, flower prints and large patch pockets, as well as long jumpers and very short skirts, are best avoided (Fig. 97).

Fig. 96

For the figure type with **large hips,** select a bodice to draw attention away from hipline. Use collars or an interesting neckline (faced with fur or velvet). Avoid narrow skirts, pockets and drapes. On the other hand, vertical seams and groups of narrow pleats for skirts are more suitable (Fig. 98).

Tall and slim women also have their problems to look well-dressed. Wear bouffant skirts, use interfacing to add fullness, soft pleats and drapes to emphasise the bust, pleated circular skirts with patch pockets and other trimmings (Fig. 99).

The overall impression should be one of pleasing harmony. The new garment should fit in well with the rest of your wardrobe. Jewellery, gloves, bags, hats, shoes and coat should also be taken into consideration, as well as the colour of hair and skin. It is best to select a basic colour scheme in grey or brown which will combine well with bright colours.

Fitting

It is very difficult trying to fit a garment on yourself and it is advisable to have another person to help you. For your first fitting, baste all the darts, shoulder seams, side seams, seams of sleeves and skirt. Turn all facings to inside, baste through the facing and seam allowance close to the seam line.

Baste and gather curve of sleeve cap according to pattern and baste sleeve seams.

Short and slender

Fig. 97

Fig. 98

Tall and slim

Fig. 99

Points to check when fitting a garment

Tie a ¾" to 1" (2 to 2·5 cm) wide ribbon or strip of fabric around your waist and pin bodice and skirt to it; this gives a better support.

Pin the front and back of bodice and skirt to the centre of your slip. This will make garment hang straight.

It is easier to locate the exact position of the pockets, if seam-lines are turned under and then pinned into position.

Place one of your buttonhole markings exactly at waistline where the stress is greatest.

Iron over basted adjustments—this will give you a better picture of how the garment will look.

When garments are lined, you will have to alter the lining as well.

Always finish the raw edges of stitched seams as you go along.

Try on bodice. Pin together centre front and opening at the side of bodice. Darts must run vertically and underarm darts must point directly towards the fullest part of the bust. Check the correct location of pocket openings and buttonholes. Side seams of skirt and bodice should run in a straight vertical position.

Wrinkles at shoulder and armhole are caused by sloping shoulders. Shoulder seams need to be lifted. Open shoulder seam and mark the amount that needs to be lifted, so that the front and back of bodice will fit smoothly. Pin the new shoulder seam together (Fig. 100).

If the garment has a vertical **bust dart** (especially for large bust) the width of the dart has to be increased. It is therefore best to have a generous seam allowance at armhole edge, in order to avoid a too narrow shoulder line. Pin dart edges over each other and fasten with a basting slip stitch.

Wrinkles at side seam of bodice: Open shoulder seam, side seam and vertical bust dart. First adjust dart and re-pin. Correct shoulder seam until it fits smoothly. Close up shoulder seam, moulding it carefully to shoulder line. Finally re-pin side seam and adjust armhole edge (Fig. 101).

In order to be able to alter garment when you try it on, cut a generous seam allowance at armhole and shoulder.

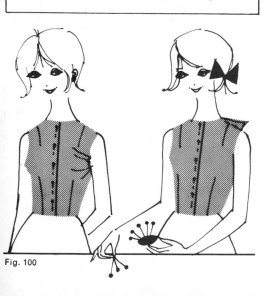

Fig. 100

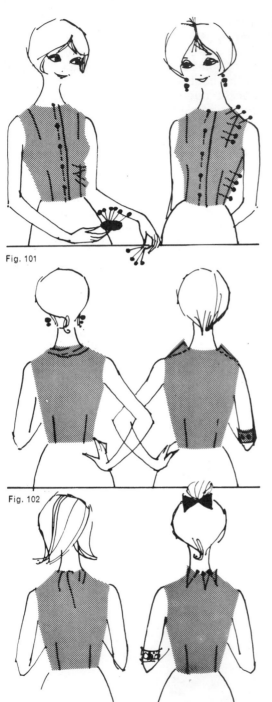

Fig. 101

Fig. 102

Fig. 103

Shoulders are especially straight and wrinkles form at neckline. Open basted shoulder seam and lift shoulder at neck edge. The narrow end of the tapered seam will be at sleeve edge. Later trim reduced size of neckline (Fig. 102).

Sometimes it is necessary to increase the width and length of the bodice dart at waistline, but be careful to keep centre front in place. Do not decrease the size of bodice too much.

A round back requires several small darts at neckline (the size of a too large neckline can also be decreased in this way). First, pin together excess fullness and by making three or four small darts distribute the fullness evenly (Fig. 103).

A neckline cut too large by mistake can be decreased in size by evenly lifting front and back of bodice, provided that a generous seam allowance has been cut at waistline.

Large busts: It is advisable to make a slanted underarm dart, moulding it to your figure contours. Again this is only possible if sufficient seam allowance has been made.

Waistline darts give back of bodice a better fit. Fold darts 3" to 4" (8 to 10 cm) from centre of back. Tapered point of dart should end in the middle of bodice back. For one-piece dresses, continue dart in a downward line and taper to point.

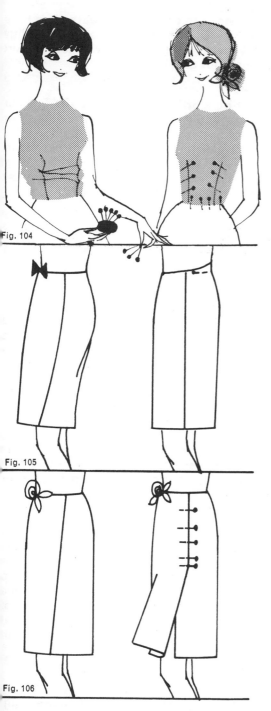

Fig. 104

Fig. 105

Fig. 106

Bulges in the back mean that bodice is too long. Unpick part of waistline seam and if necessary side seam and centre back seam, smooth out wrinkles and pin together according to body contours. Shorten waistline, so that bodice at the back fits smoothly (Fig. 104).

A straight skirt is more difficult to fit than a full one. A straight skirt should fit well. First correct the waistline seam. Straight skirts have a tendency to sway back and this causes a few shallow wrinkles. Lift and ease fabric up into the waistband at the back until wrinkles disappear (Fig. 105). It is important to check the fit of the waistband; make sure that it is not too snug or too loose. The skirt must not be too tight over the hips. Waistline darts should give the necessary width.

Check the side seams of your skirt: They should run in a straight and vertical line. If this is not the case, unpick the side seam and pin the folded edge of seam of the front of skirt to the back of skirt (Fig. 106).

Gored skirts consisting of panels, should also be checked for straight seams. If necessary cut waistline edge slightly deeper.

Circular skirts: Uneven distribution of folds is corrected by slightly lifting the skirt waistline in places.

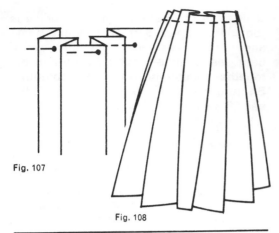

Fig. 107

Fig. 108

Skirts with unpressed pleats often have an uneven hemline. It is enough to slightly lift the underside of pleat at top of skirt (Figs. 107 and 108).

Fitting a difficult set-in sleeve: To help in fitting a difficult set-in sleeve, a basting stitch is used to mark the straight length-wise and crosswise grains at the cap of the sleeve, thus forming a cross. When fitting the sleeve, the vertical basting stitch must match shoulder seam (Fig. 109).

For your first fitting baste sleeve seams and gather fullness at sleeve top, turn under armhole edge, pin sleeve over arm-hole (Fig. 110).

For your second fitting baste the finished sleeve into the armhole. To obtain a more exact fit, try on garment, turn seam allow-ance of sleeve to inside, pin over armhole and fasten with a slip stitch.

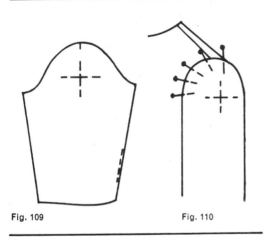

Fig. 109   Fig. 110

Long narrow sleeves: Clip seam allow-ance at bend of elbow, to avoid puckering at the seamline (Fig. 111). Mark and pin the required length of the sleeve at your first fitting. Have sleeve completed for your second fitting.

When setting sleeve into armhole, make sure that you have sufficient fullness for movement. If wrinkles appear at the upper part of sleeve, move sleeve cap slightly towards the back and at the same time lift the front part of the sleeve cap. Sleeve pulls and wrinkles at the top. Let out the sleeve seam and ease more width into the sleeve cap.

For your second fitting baste-stitch sleeve in armhole in case you have to make slight adjustments (Fig. 112).

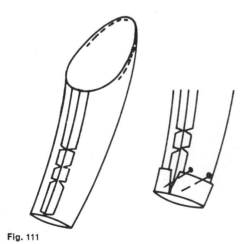

Fig. 111

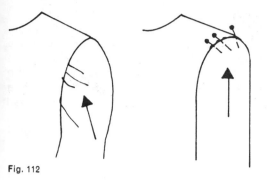

Fig. 112

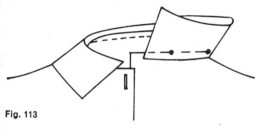

Fig. 113

Attach collar to garment by basting it right side up to neckline. The neckline must fit smoothly without gaping and pulling. Exceptions are stand-away collars. Here the neckline edge surrounds the neck at an even distance. Check the fit of collar. Bind cut edges with a bias strip.

Two-piece collar: Pin and baste edge of under collar section to neckline only (Fig. 113).

Detachable collars: Bind the neckline with a bias strip or ready-made bias binding. Slip-stitch collar to neckline.

Prepare the garment for the second fitting. Now put the garment on. There should be hardly any alterations necessary. Only slight faults at sleeves and collar may have to be corrected. Now chalk-mark hemline.

A skirt marker will enable you to mark the hemline yourself. If you do not possess a skirt marker, ask a friend to chalk-mark your dress length by placing a long ruler or sleeve board on the floor. Instead of chalk you can use pins to mark the hemline (Fig. 114).

Now give the garment the finishing touch— oversew raw edges of seam allowance, sew on buttons. Give the completed garment a final pressing.

Fig. 114

Floating Panels

Panels are loose hanging or lightly bunched pieces of fabric, used mostly on elegant garments. The floating panels are attached to the shoulder or belt of the dress, emphasising each graceful movement of the wearer (Fig. 115). Choose a delicate fabric that will drape nicely.

Fig. 115

Flounce

Cut the flounce in circular form. Cut the circle open on the straight grain. Seam flounce sections together. Neaten the outer edge of the joined sections with a zigzag stitch, using Gütermann Sew-all thread. Clip the inner edge at intervals. With right sides together, stitch to garment in a straight line.

When a flounce is applied to washable fabrics, stitch bias binding to inner edge of flounce. Stitch to garment, turn under free edge of binding and slip-stitch into place (Fig. 116).

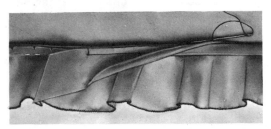

Fig. 116

French Tack

A French tack is used to hold two fabric edges together loosely.

Make several stitches across the two fabric sections. Work over thread strands with blanket stitches. Pass the needle always through the preceding loop and pull the thread through (Fig. 117).

French tacks are often used to attach the lining to a coat at the hemline.

Fig. 117

Fringe

Apply the fringe to the selvage edge of two layers of fabric. Wind the yarn around a piece of cardboard. Cut the yarn at one edge in order to obtain even length strands. Insert a crochet hook into the finished fabric edge, and, with the hook, pick up cut strands at the uncut edge and pull through the fabric. Pull the cut ends through the loop to fasten (Fig. 118).

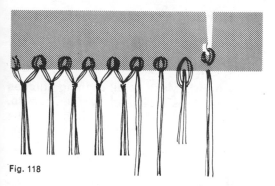

Fig. 118

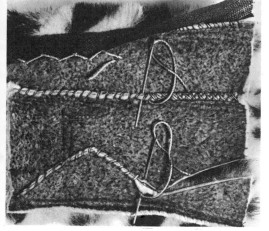

Fig. 119

Fur

Small fur collars or fur trimmings can be made by joining small fur pieces together. For cutting, use a razor blade instead of scissors; this is to avoid damaging the hair of the fur. Raise the fur slightly from the cutting surface and cut only the skin with a sharp blade. Some types of fur can be joined in a straight line, whereas smooth types of fur are better joined if they are cut in zigzag or wavy lines. Use a furrier's three-sided needle and join the edges of the skin with small overhand stitches. Fur is cut without a seam allowance. Push the hair out of the seam with the point of the needle as you join the edges. Fluff up fur after joining is completed.

Finish the outside edges of the fur with tape. Place the edges of the tape matching the cut edge of the skin. Join tape and skin with an overhand stitch and turn the tape back to the skin side. If the fur has been backed with cotton padding, sew the tape with herring-bone stitches to the backing (Fig. 119).

Fur collar or trimming is attached to the fabric section with a slip stitch. Slip-stitch the edges of the fabric to the tape of the fur collar.

Fur border: Use a strip of fur for edging a neckline, an opening or hemline of a garment. The lined piece of fur is stitched to the finished edge of the neckline or hem (Fig. 120).

Fig. 120   Compact with broad hips

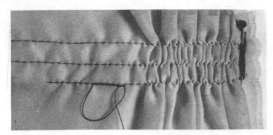

Fig. 121

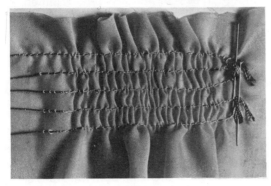

Fig. 122

Fig. 123

Gathering

Gathering can be done by hand or by machine.

1. **By hand:** Make small running stitches on the lines indicated by your pattern. Pull up the thread, and distribute the fullness to the desired amount (Fig. 121).

2. **By machine:** Adjust the stitch regulator on your machine to a $\frac{1}{4}''$ (5 mm) stitch. Make two or more rows of evenly-spaced stitching. Draw up the bobbin thread and distribute the fullness to the required amount (Fig. 122).

Secure one end of the drawn-up thread by winding around a pin, which is placed at right angles to the stitching.

Knot thread ends at the beginning and the end of each line of stitching, or sew a small pleat on the wrong side of the fabric to secure thread ends.

If the gathering is done by hand, make the running stitches by keeping the needle in the fabric, while the left hand moves the fabric quickly up and down in front of the point of the needle (Fig. 123).

Elastic thread can be used for gathering children's dresses, nightgowns, etc. (Fig. 124).

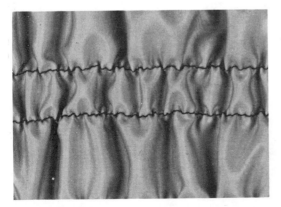

Fig. 124

Fig. 125

Godet

A godet is a wedge-shaped fabric section, set in a straight skirt to give added width at the hem. Reinforce the point of the godet with a piece of fabric (Fig. 125).

Fig. 126

Gored or Circular Skirt

The basic design is a circle or a circle made from several gored sections of fabric. The circular or gored skirt fits closely over the hips and is wide at the hem. Allow the skirt to hang for a day or two before making the hem. This will help bias edges to stretch and will prevent an uneven hem (Fig. 126).

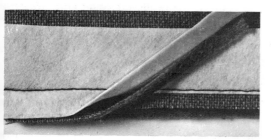

Fig. 127

Grading (Seam Layering)

Also sometimes called layering. It is a method used to eliminate bulk from seams, especially when several layers of fabric lie over one another, making seam edges unnecessarily bulky. Always cut the seam allowance of interfacings close to the seam. Trim one seam allowance narrower than the other for a flat finish (Fig. 127).

Grain Line

Grain is the direction of the fabric thread which runs parallel and at right angles to the selvage. See also CUTTING (page 28).

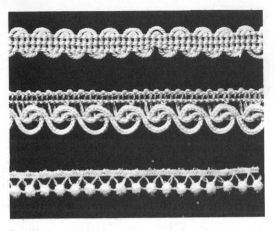

Fig. 128

Guipure

A raised cotton lace trimming in the form of continuous motifs, the traditional pattern being a flower or daisy design giving an embroidered effect when applied (Fig. 128).

Gütermann Sewing Threads

Gütermann is a well-known sewing thread company, with factories in eight European countries. The name of Gütermann guarantees a sewing thread of unsurpassed first-class quality.

Gütermann Sew-all thread is the correct choice for hand or machine sewing, where elasticity, permanent extension, colour fastness and high abrasion resistance are required. For use on all fabrics, particularly synthetic, blended and stretch, it is a fine, strong, durable thread resulting in a neat, fine seam. Available in a large colour range.

Gütermann Sew-all thread is available in three sizes: 100 m (110 yds) standard length reels, 250 m (275 yds) dressmaker length reels and 500 m (547 yds) economy length cops.

Gütermann Twist, designed specifically for decorative stitching, is ideal for any job where strength is important. It can be used for all buttonholing, button sewing looping and saddle stitching. Available in a large range of colours on a 30 m (33 yds) reel.

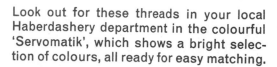

Look out for these threads in your local Haberdashery department in the colourful 'Servomatik', which shows a bright selection of colours, all ready for easy matching.

Hand Embroidery

Embroidery stitches are often used to give an attractive finish to a garment (Fig. 129).

Cross stitch: Work diagonal stitches from left to right, then go back the way you came and make the second half of crosses over the first stitches. Always re-insert needle in the same hole from the previous stitch.

Herring-bone stitch: This stitch is worked from left to right horizontally. The thread is carried diagonally to the next stitch.

Chain stitch: Work the chain stitch from top to bottom. Bring needle to right side of fabric. Insert needle at almost the same point, bring needle out making the stitch the length of the loop, keeping the thread under the needle point.

Lazy daisy stitch: This is an elongated chain stitch. Arrange the chain stitch to form the petals of a daisy or arrange in a staggered line.

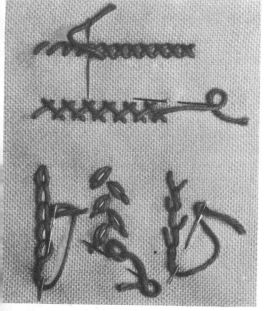

Fig. 129

Feather stitch: Work from top to bottom. The needle is inserted diagonally each side of the centre line alternately, keeping the thread under the needle point.

For all hand embroidery, use Gütermann Twist on heavy materials, Gütermann Sew-all thread on fine fabrics.

Fig. 130

Hand-stitched Seam

This particular hand stitch is used for seams on delicate or transparent fabrics. Take two or three short running stitches, then a back stitch to secure the running stitches; continue in this manner (Fig. 130).

Hand Stitches

Hand stitches are stitches executed by hand.

Running stitch: This is a tiny stitch about $\frac{1}{8}''$ (3 mm) in length. Pass the needle in and out of the fabric before pulling the thread through. Stitches appear the same on both sides of the fabric. Running stitches are also used for basting.

Guide basting: This is a version of the running stitch, except that the stitches are longer. (See Running stitch.) Take a long stitch on the upper side of the fabric and a short stitch on the underside. Use this stitch to mark contours and construction symbols on fabrics (Fig. 131).

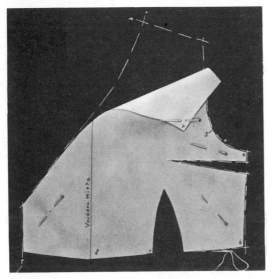

Fig. 131

Diagonal basting: This stitch is used to hold several layers of fabric together, for example quilting. Stitch from top to bottom diagonally through the fabric and then stitch through the fabric at right angles (Fig. 132). Diagonal basting is similar to padding stitch. Padding stitches are shorter and have to be executed with great care. See PADDING STITCH page 84.

Fig. 132

Herring-bone stitch: Used as a decorative embroidery stitch or it can be used to hold down two edges of a hem or a facing, when it is difficult to turn under the raw edges. Herring-bone stitches worked close together are also used as a seam finish (Fig. 133). The herring-bone stitch is worked from left to right. Insert needle and

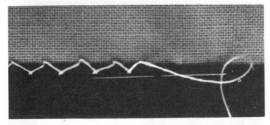

Fig. 133

Fig. 134

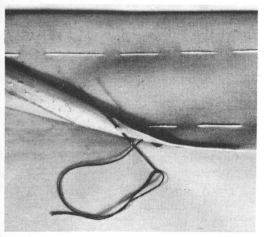

Fig. 135

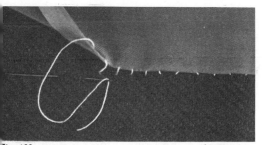

Fig. 136

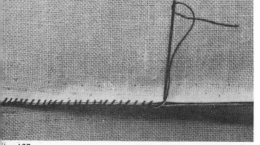

Fig 137

with a back stitch pick up a few threads on the top layer of the fabric and then pick up a thread diagonally in the lower layer of the fabric, so that stitches cross each other.

Back stitch: Start with a running stitch, then insert the needle back at the start of the first stitch and bring it out one stitch ahead. The stitch is twice as long at the underside as it is on the top. Repeat this stitch for a continuous seam (Fig. 134).

Invisible hemming stitch: Work from right to left. With needle pick up one or two threads of the garment underneath the turned-up hem, then pick up a thread of the hem diagonally above. The hemming stitch has a slight slant (Fig. 135).

Blind hemming stitch: This is really a slip stitch, used when stitching should be invisible. Slide needle along upper fold of fabric. Bring needle down perpendicularly and pick up a few threads on the lower fabric section. Bring needle up again and slide through upper fold. Do not pull stitches too tightly (Fig. 136).

Overhand stitch: Overhand stitch is used to join two fabric sections with selvage edges. Baste selvage edges right sides together. Oversew with small stitches. Keep stitches close together. Do not pull thread too tightly (Fig. 137).

Hems

Hems should be as inconspicuous as possible and range in depth from $1\frac{1}{2}''$ to $3''$ (4 to 8 cm). Mark the hemline the required depth and turn up hem. Baste hem into place about $\frac{3}{4}''$ (2 cm) from the fold line. Measure the required depth of the hem from fold line and mark with chalk around the entire skirt. Trim hem to an even width. Hems may be finished in a number of ways.

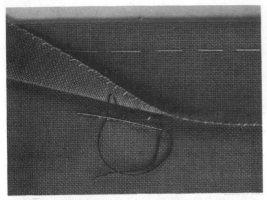

Fig. 138

For light-weight fabrics turn under raw edge for about ⅜″ (1 cm), or finish edge with oversewing or zigzag stitch, then baste and slip-stitch hem into place. With needle pick up a few threads of the fabric beneath the hem, bring needle out and make a stitch through the fold of the fabric or slightly below the oversewing or zigzag stitching (Fig. 138).

For heavy fabrics bind the raw edges with bias binding or seam tape and slip-stitch to the garment (Fig. 139).

Fig. 139

Cut the raw edge with pinking shears, if the fabric is very heavy or bulky. Strengthen cut edge with a row of straight machine stitching about ¼″ (6 mm) from the cut edge. Slip-stitch hem to the garment (with Gütermann Sew-all thread) (Fig. 140), or attach hem from left to right with herring-bone stitches.

For a less conspicuous hem, neaten edge with a blanket stitch and slip-stitch hem to the garment. With needle pick up blanket stitch thread and not fabric threads (Fig. 141). Insert the needle, picking up blanket stitch, then pick up thread of garment beneath.

Fig. 140

The types of hem just described do not have turned under edges and have therefore the advantage that the point of the iron can be taken under the neatened edges, preventing any impression of the upper edge showing on the right side of the garment, as can easily happen with some types of fabric.

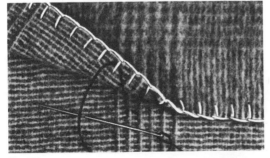

Fig. 141

Faced hem: If there is not enough fabric to make a hem, a strip of lining about 2″ (5 cm) wide is cut on the bias and used to face the bottom of the garment. Sew the strip to the bottom of the garment with right sides together, allowing for a ¼″ (6 mm) seam allowance. Press seam open

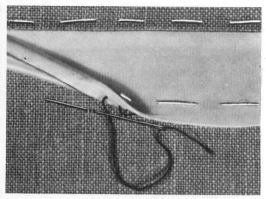

Fig. 142

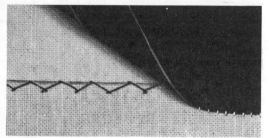

Fig. 143

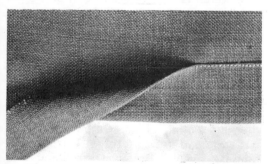

Fig. 144

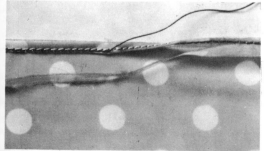

Fig. 145

Turn the facing and edge of hemline to inside. The free edge of the facing is turned under and slip-stitched to the garment (Fig. 142). For a narrow skirt, use wide seam binding instead of bias facing.

Lining attached to hemline: Attach the hem with herring-bone stitches to the wrong side of the garment. The herring-bone stitch (see HERRING-BONE STITCH page 54) is worked from left to right, keeping thread fairly loose (Fig. 143). To avoid impression of hem edge showing through, insert the needle $\frac{1}{8}''$ (3 mm) above and below hem edge.

Machine-stitched hem: The hem is turned under twice. Both turnings are exactly the same width. Machine-stitch close to the edge of the hem (Fig. 144). Straight fabric edges will lie especially flat, if the first turning is wide enough to meet the fold line.

The hem is usually stitched on the wrong side of the garment, except for a decorative hem. Here a wide hem is turned to the outside of the garment and machine-stitched with Gütermann Twist close to the folded edge.

WHIPPED HEM see ROLLED HEM page 104.

Braid binding edges see BRAIDS page 13.

Narrow machine-stitched hems give a nearly invisible edge finish for dresses made from sheer fabrics. Use a straight machine stitch or a tiny zigzag stitch. Turn under raw edge $\frac{3}{8}''$ (1 cm) to wrong side, machine-stitch close to folded edge, taking care not to pull the fabric. Trim raw edge close to stitching, fold the stitched edge once more to the wrong side and machine a second time close to the folded edge (Fig. 145).

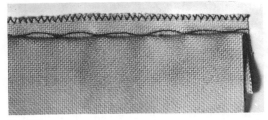

Fig. 146

Fig. 147

Fig. 148

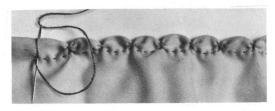

Fig. 149

Hem executed automatically: For coloured peasant skirts where the hem should not be visible, use the automatic blind stitch hemmer attachment or scallop stitch for slip hemming. Adjust and lengthen stitch according to your requirements. Finish raw edge of hem with a zigzag stitch. Fold hem back against the outside of the garment, the folded edge of the skirt should be about $\frac{1}{2}''$ (1 cm) from upper hem edge. The curved or scalloped seam runs along the wrong side of the turned-up hem and only the point of each curve or scallop picks up one or two threads of the fabric on the folded edge of the garment. Stitches are invisible on the right side of the fabric, except on sheer fabrics. Use matching coloured thread (Fig. 146).

Hem, bonded: On delicate fabrics where stitches can be seen on the right side of the garment, the hem should be pressed on. There is a non-woven material available which is very fine and can be ironed on, on both sides, i.e. Vilene. Cut a strip the width of the hem, place between the hem allowance and the garment. Press on with an iron (Fig. 147).

Hems for circular pattern pieces: Hems for gored and circular skirts should be narrow to eliminate bulk. Oversew the raw edge of the hem. Gather along the cut edge and draw up thread, distributing fullness evenly. Press gathers flat and secure this edge to garment with slipstitch, keeping tension of stitches quite loose (Fig. 148).

Hem, decorative: This type of hem is used as a decorative finish for collars, cuffs, lingerie and babies' clothes. The shell edge is worked by hand. Make two turnings about 1″ (2·5 cm) wide. With running stitches sew down hem for about $\frac{1}{2}''$ to 1″ (1 to 2·5 cm), then take one or two stitches over the edge (Fig. 149). Draw thread tight. Repeat.

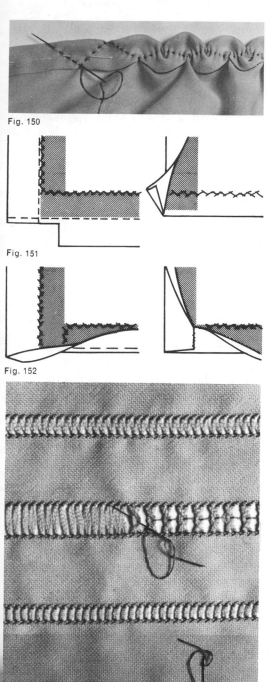

Fig. 150

Fig. 151

Fig. 152

Fig. 153

For another type of decorative hem, fold hem to the outside of the garment. Make tiny running stitches diagonally from edge to edge. Draw up thread to form shells of uniform size (Fig. 150).

Hem with facing: Hems with facing are worked for jackets and coats depending on the fabric (Figs. 151 and 152). The hems are often interfaced to prevent stretching of the lower edges. Herring-bone stitch interfacing to the garment. Turn up hem over the interfacing. Turn facing to inside over hem.

If fabric is heavy and bulky, grade the facing hem for a flat finish (Fig. 151).

For light-weight fabric, stitch hem in position the entire length including the facing, then turn the facing to inside. The lower edge of the facing should never protrude beyond the hemline. Slip-stitch inner edge of facing as inconspicuously as possible to hem, using tiny stitches. Turn under raw edges of inner edge of facing and slip-stitch to hem or leave unfinished (Fig. 152).

For bed and table linen, make an 'envelope corner' see MITRED CORNER page 71.

Hemstitch

This decorative stitch is worked on straight grain lines. The lengthwise and crosswise threads of the fabric must run at right angles to each other. Draw out the required number of crosswise threads from fabric. The remaining lengthwise threads are grouped together at both edges with hand stitches (Fig. 153). Pass the needle under a few of the threads, draw the threads around them, take a stitch to the right of the threads and bring out the needle to the front by pulling thread tight. Continue by encircling the next group of threads.

Hand hemstitching looks even more decorative, when thread groups are alternated in zigzag fashion or interlaced through the centre with a thread. The edges of the drawn out sections can be fastened quickly and permanently with a machine zigzag stitch.

A different type of hemstitching is faggoting, which is the decorative joining of two finished edges. See FAGGOTING page 39.

Hooks and Eyes

Hooks and eyes should always be sewn to two layers of fabrics, because stitches should never show on the right side of the garment. Turned-under edges should be reinforced with seam tape or a piece of interfacing. Sew hooks about $\frac{1}{8}''$ (3 mm) from the edge of the closing; the curve of the eye protrudes from outer edge of the closing.

Fig. 154

Attach hooks and eyes by sewing through the holes. Secure the hook end with a few extra overhand stitches. Hooks are sometimes attached to the garment by pushing the hook through the fabric (Fig. 154).

With an overhand stitch, stitch around the holes using matching thread and instead of using eyes, make thread eyes with matching thread. This method makes the fastening inconspicuous.

On waistbands, sew the hooks close to the overlap and the eye to the underlap.

For a more secure fastening, change the position of hooks and eyes. Attach a hook and an eye to the overlap and an eye and a hook to the underlap (Fig. 155). Cover the holes attaching the hooks and eyes to the

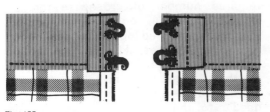

Fig. 155

Fig. 156

garment with seam tape or a strip of lining.

Inserting Lace or Braid

Stitch the lace or braid to the right side of the fabric. Cut away fabric on the wrong side under the insertion. Press the fabric edges away from the insertion. Using a zigzag stitch sew once more over both edges of the insertion. Trim the fabric edges close to the stitching (Fig. 156).

If you want to insert lace between gathered fabric sections, do not cut the fabric into strips but leave it in one piece. Gather the fabric to the desired fullness, now baste the lace along the gathering lines and cut away the fabric underneath the insertion. Sew with a small zigzag stitch once more over both insertion seam lines.

Instruction Labels for Textiles

Dry Cleaning

A Cotton or linen: use ordinary solvents.

P Colour-fast cotton, linen and rayon: use perchlorethylene or benzine.

F Nylon, acrylic, polyester, etc.: use benzine only.

⊗ Sensitive fabrics: do not dry clean.

Ironing

🔲 Cool (120° C): Acrylic, nylon, acetate, triacetate, polyester.

🔲 Warm (160° C): Polyester mixtures, wool.

🔲 Hot (210° C): Rayon or modified rayon, cotton, linen.

⊠ Do not iron.

 White cotton and linen articles without special finishes.

 Cotton, linen or rayon articles without special finishes where colours are fast at 60 C.

 White nylon; white polyester/cotton.

 Coloured nylon; polyester, cotton and rayon articles with special finishes; acrylic/cotton; coloured polyester/cotton.

 Cotton, linen or rayon articles where colours are fast at 40 C but not at 60 C.

 Acrylics; acetate and triacetate, including mixtures with wool; polyester/wool blends.

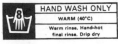 Wool, including blankets and wool mixtures with cotton or rayon. Silk.

 Washable pleated garments containing acrylics, nylon, polyester or triacetate glass fibre fabrics.

DO NOT WASH Would normally have a dry-cleaning label to indicate dry cleaning only.

Inverted Pleat with Underlay

The pleat is set into a seam with a wide seam allowance. With this type of pleat, the depth of the pleat is set in separately.

The short inner pleat should be as long as the inverted pleat. Cut a rectangle from skirt fabric, the width and the length plus hem. Allow an extra 1″ (2·5 cm) to secure upper edge of the underlay. Place the rectangle over the seam, matching hemlines. Machine-stitch to seam allowance of skirt. Make a curved seam towards the upper edge to prevent tearing. At hemline clip the seam allowance diagonally to prevent seam allowance from protruding. Oversew the raw edges of seam allowance (Fig. 157).

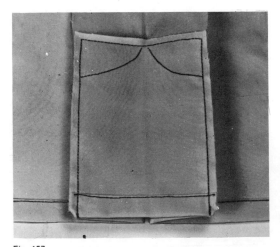

Fig. 157

If skirt seam allowance is narrow, cut the underlay accordingly wider in order to obtain the required depth of the pleat. Stitch to seam allowance of the skirt. Attach a piece of lining material, reaching from the upper edge of underlay to the waistline.

Kimono Sleeves

A sleeve cut in one with the bodice. A gusset may be inserted if greater freedom is needed. See SLEEVES page 121.

Lace

Lace applied to fabric: Narrow lace edging is gathered by drawing up a basting thread through the straight edge of the lace. Valenciennes lace usually has a draw thread through the upper edge of the lace.

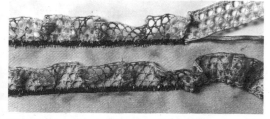

Fig. 158

Make a narrow hem with one or two turnings on the edge of the garment. Baste the lace to the hem edge. Lace can also be attached at the same time as the narrow hem is made with the special narrow hemmer foot of your sewing machine. Sew the lace to the garment with tiny whipping or satin stitches, keeping stitches close together. Or machine to garment with a closely set zigzag stitch.

For groups of lace frills, mark the individual spaces with a basting thread. Sew the partly gathered lace to the edge of the fabric (Fig. 158).

Joining lace: Cut single motifs out of lace fabrics. These motifs are pieced together. The connecting bars are worked by hand (Fig. 159).

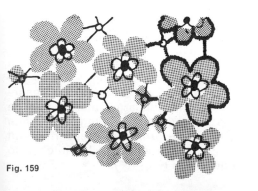

Fig. 159

See INSERTING LACE page 61.

Fig. 160

Lingerie Strap Holders

Strap holders keep slipping lingerie straps in place. Cut a piece of seam binding or ribbon about 2″ (5 cm) long. Fold in half crosswise, and sew one half to the inside shoulder seamline with opening towards neck edge. Sew one half of a snap to the fastened end of ribbon, sew the other half to the loose end (Fig. 160).

Linings

Linings are cut with a generous seam allowance from the same pattern as the garment. Shoulder, sleeve and side seams are machine-stitched with Gütermann Sew-all thread. To attach lining, put on garment wrong side out, or place on a dressmaker's dummy or a coathanger.

Sew coat tab with Gütermann Twist to collar seam line, before lining is pinned to the side seams under armhole and centre back at neckline (Fig. 161). Fold a lengthwise pleat at centre back of lining, to ensure enough freedom of movement.

The back pleat is secured with a few herring-bone stitches as shown (Fig. 161).

Clip-cut edge of front lining to prevent stretching, turn under seam allowance and pin to the front facing. Slip-stitch to garment with Gütermann Sew-all thread (Fig. 162).

Baste lining to armhole. Slip lining over sleeves. Slip-stitch lining to facing or turned-up hem of lower sleeve edge. The lining should overlap slightly; the extra length will prevent drawing. About 4″ to $4\frac{1}{2}$″ (10 to 11 cm) from the sleeve cap, baste lining to sleeve with large stitches, remove basting threads after lining has been slip-stitched to armhole. The shrunk-out sleeve cap of the lining is slip-stitched to shoulder seam (Fig. 163).

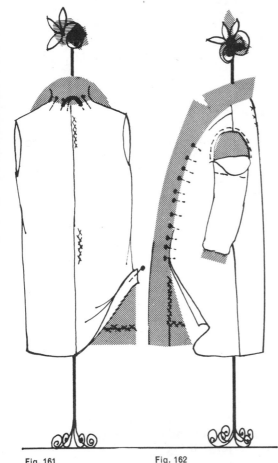
Fig. 161   Fig. 162

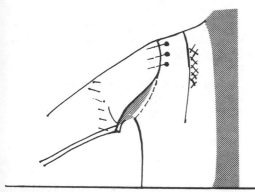

Fig. 163

Fig. 164

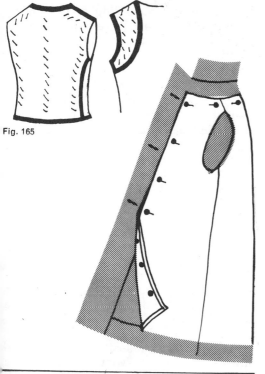

Fig. 165

Fig. 166

Loose coat lining: The lining of a coat need not be slip-stitched to the hem. Fasten lining to hem with French tacks or pieces of seam tape. They are attached between the coat and the lining (Fig. 164). See also FRENCH TACK (page 48).

The lining of a jacket should be cut slightly longer at the lower edge. When turned under, the lower edge of the lining should overlap the hem of the jacket.

Interlinings are used for added warmth, for example quilting or a lining with wool wadding. Cut according to coat or jacket pattern. The interlining should be half to three-quarters of the length of the garment and is sewn between the top cloth and the lining. The cutting edges of the interlining should be given a flat finish with bias binding, seam tape or braid (Fig. 165).

A Button-in wool lining is fastened to the coat or jacket with buttons or snap fasteners. The button-in lining has no sleeves and is left loose at the bottom. Finish the outside edges of the lining with bias binding or braid (Fig. 166).

For children's coats or jackets use large patent snap fasteners. Push the holding pins of the snap fasteners through the facing and lining, bend them down and press them firmly to the wrong side of the coat.

Linings for Skirts

The shape of a narrow skirt is retained, if it is lined with taffeta (Fig. 167). The lining is cut from the same pattern piece as the skirt, the width and the darts must be the same. The finished length of the lining should be shorter than the skirt. For greater freedom of movement leave the side seams at the bottom of the lining open (b).

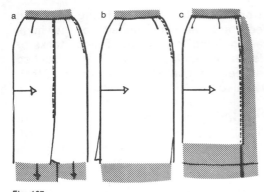

Fig. 167

To line a skirt in the wrap-over style, overlap the lining at centre back and leave open at the bottom (*a*).

For skirts made from a **firmly woven fabric,** a partial lining at the back of the skirt is enough to prevent sagging. The piece of lining is attached to the side seams by hand. As the lining is only knee-high, side slits are not necessary (*c*).

In general it is easier to press a skirt with a loose hanging lining. Press the wrong side of a skirt with the lining attached to side seams by sliding the ironing board between the lining and the skirt, place a damp cloth under the wrong side of the skirt and steam-press on the right side.

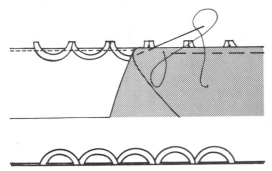

Fig. 168

Loops

Loops make an interesting fastening for dresses and blouses. Make a narrow tube from the dress material. The size of the loops depends on the size of the button. Cut loops to correct length to fit easily over buttons, plus seam allowance. Sew them by hand to the right side of the garment along the opening. The cut edges of the loops lie towards the opening edge.

Cover the loops with a piece of facing. Stitch along the opening edge and turn facing to inside of garment (Fig. 168).

Continuous loops (Fig. 169) are used on finished garment edges. Fold a piece of fabric tubing the length of the loops and pin to the edge of the opening. The fold line of the fabric tubing is attached with an overhand stitch to the garment. Stitches should not show on the right side of the garment.

Thread loops: These are invisible. Work with Gütermann Twist. Sew several strands of thread the size of the loop to

Fig. 169

the edge of the opening. Work blanket or loop stitches over the thread strands, keeping stitches close together, or just wrap the thread tightly around the strands of the loop.

Loops which lie flat along the edge of a garment are even less noticeable and are best worked with Gütermann Sew-all thread.

Machine Embroidery

With a modern automatic sewing machine, embroidering is as simple as sewing, when using zigzag stitches or by setting the regulator knob for a satin scallop stitch (Fig. 170).

As each machine has its special features, consult your sewing machine manual.

Use Gütermann Sew-all thread on fine fabrics and Gütermann Twist on heavy materials.

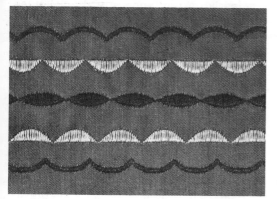

Fig. 170

Marking of Fabric

Outlines and symbols have to be transferred from pattern to the fabric. There are several methods of marking, so select the one most suitable for the fabric being used (Fig. 171 a–d). All the markings on pattern pieces should be transferred to the wrong side of the fabric. The different methods are outlined as follows:

1. On linen or cotton fabrics with a special finish, use a tracing wheel to trace the outlines of the pattern (a). Mark the outlines of pattern pieces, construction symbols and straight lines, darts, etc. with tracing wheel. The tracing wheel will leave small pin-prick-like impressions on both sides of double thickness

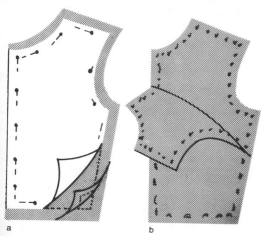

a b

Fig. 171

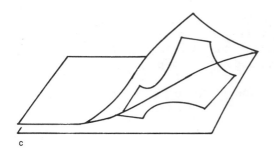

c

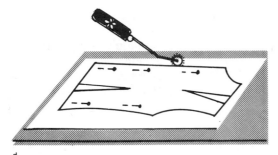

d

Fig. 171

of fabric. As these impressions soon disappear, it is advisable to mark over them with tailor's chalk.

2. The use of tailor's tacks is recommended for firmly woven fabrics (*b*). See TAILOR'S TACKS page 127.

3. Dressmaker's carbon paper. With carbon paper, both wrong sides of double thickness of fabric will be marked at the same time (*c*). Use carbon in a contrasting colour, so markings will show more clearly on the fabric. For double thickness of fabric (fold fabric right sides together), place one sheet of carbon paper face up under lower layer of fabric, place a second sheet face down to upper fabric layer.

Place pattern piece over carbon and upper fabric layer and trace around pattern with tracing wheel, marking symbols and straight lines (d). Test on a piece of fabric to see that carbon colour is suitable for the type of fabric being used. This method is not suitable for delicate colours or loosely woven fabrics. See also TRACING WITH CARBON PAPER page 131.

4. Use tailor's chalk on heavy materials. Always mark on the wrong side of the fabric. Transfer outlines and symbols to one side of the fabric, place the wrong side of the second fabric section over it and apply pressure so that markings appear on the other side. Chalk marks vanish quickly, therefore baste over markings immediately.

Measurements, how to take

Knowing your correct measurements is important when choosing your pattern. Sizes for adult clothing are given according to bust measurements.

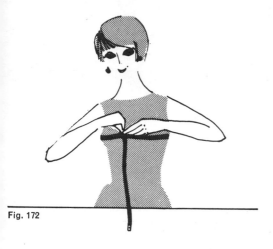

Fig. 172

The necessary ease allowance is already included in the pattern measurement, to ensure a comfortable fit.

Measure bust over the fullest part without drawing tapemeasure too tight. The tapemeasure must lie over the shoulder blades at the back (Fig. 172).

Always keep in mind that figure types with the same bust measurements need not necessarily have the same measurements elsewhere. The importance of taking the correct measurements can never be stressed enough.

The most important measurements are shown in Fig. 173:

1. Neck width

2. Bust
   (measured well over shoulder blades)

3. Waist

4. Hips
   (about 8″ (20 cm) beneath waist)

5. Front width

6. Back width

7. Front waist length

8. Back waist length

9. Side length

10. Shoulder length
    (press a ruler under armpit measure from tip of ruler over and around top of shoulder)

11. Shoulder width

12. Upper arm circumference

Fig. 173

Measurement Chart

Measurements of:

1. Neck width					
2. Bust					
3. Waist					
4. Hips					
5. Front width					
6. Back width					
7. Front waist length					
8. Back waist length					
9. Side length					
10. Shoulder length					
11. Shoulder width					
12. Upper arm circumference					
13. Sleeve length					
14. Elbow circumference					
15. Wrist circumference					
16. Front skirt length					
17. Front length waistline at front to floor					
18. Back length waistline at back to floor					
19. Bust depth					

13. Sleeve length

14. Elbow circumference

15. Wrist circumference

16. Front skirt length

17. Front length
    (waist at front to floor)

18. Back length
    (waistline at back to floor)

19. Bust depth
    (from neck edge to fullest part of the body)

Mitred Corners

Mitred corner hem: Fold corner in a right angle, right sides together, diagonally. Stitch along the diagonal crease, trim to within $\frac{1}{4}''$ (6 mm) of the seam. Turn the hem to inside (Fig. 174 *a*).

There is also another method. Turn under the raw edges of the hem and stitch, turn again and attach hem by hand to the garment. Hems on heavy-weight fabrics should be attached with a herring-bone stitch. Sew the lining over the hem edge.

Mitred corners cut and hand-finished: They are especially suitable for linen and curtains, because they lie flat and they are very durable. Turn under the hem allowance and press. Open out the pressed hem allowance. Fold mitre at the corner diagonally to the edges of the hems. Mark the mitre fold line with a tracing wheel or press fold line with an iron. Trim off corner diagonally, about $\frac{1}{4}''$ (6 mm) from the fold line. Turn under edge $\frac{1}{4}''$ (6 mm) on the diagonal fold line to the inside. Turn the hems to the inside again, and slip-stitch edges of mitre together (Fig. 174 *b*).

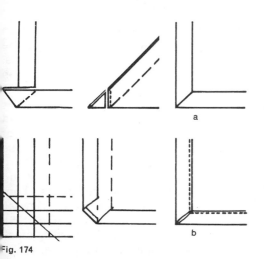

a

b

Fig. 174

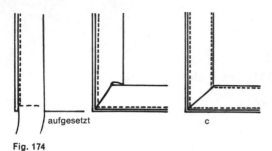

aufgesetzt   c

Fig. 174

Corners with facing: Turn under the seam allowance of the facing. Turn under the raw edges of the hem. Stitch facing to garment, wrong sides together. At the corners fold a diagonal crease and continue stitching along the edges. The corner of the facing will fold back on itself (Fig. 174 c).

Neck Openings

Openings consist of an overlap and an underlap. They are worked in double thickness of fabric with the interfacing sandwiched between the garment fabric and the facing. Make the buttonholes in the overlap and sew the buttons with Gütermann Twist to the underlap or underside of the closing.

For a concealed fastening, work the left side of the opening as usual. Baste interfacing to the facing and also to the right side of the opening. Line both sections separately with a piece of lining material, the length of the opening, using Gütermann Sew-all thread.

Before turning lining to the right side, trim interfacing seam allowance close to the seam. Clip seam allowance at intervals. Press the seam open. Make buttonholes in the facing section.

With right sides facing, baste the lined facing about $\frac{1}{8}''$ (3 mm) from edge of opening. Stitch facing to garment across the top and the bottom of opening. Turn facing to inside. Make a row of basting stitches along the edge and press. Topstitch edge with Gütermann Sew-all thread, if indicated on pattern (Fig. 175). Attach facing to garment by making small bar tacks between each buttonhole.

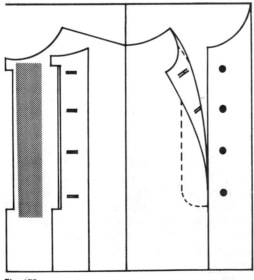

Fig. 175

Fig. 176 a   b

Fig. 176

Facing cut in one with the garment:
The overlap and the facing for the right front section is cut in one. The underlap and facing is cut in one with the left front section. The centre front seam of the bodice coincides with the edge of the closing. Apply a light-weight interfacing to underlap and overlap, to the wrong side of the garment. Place the interlining or interfacing right to the fold line of the facing. For a neat finish, extend the interfacing along the centre seam to the waistline. This is advisable when using a loosely woven fabric (Fig. 176 a). If the garment has piped buttonholes, make the buttonholes through the garment and interfacing before the facing is applied. Turn the cut in one facing to the outside of the garment. Machine-stitch across the upper edge of the opening, extend stitches to the point where collar is joined to the neckline. Stitch the lower end diagonally up to the centre seam. Cut into the seam allowance diagonally at the end of the seam. Trim away seam allowance of interfacing close to the seam, or up to the fold line respectively (Fig. 176 b). Turn facing to inside and press open centre seam. Finish buttonholes by cutting through the facing the same length as the buttonhole opening. The edges of the facing are turned under and slip-stitched to the line of stitching, or make worked buttonholes through the garment, interfacing and facing. Lap right side over the left side and slip-stitch the lower edges together, or stitch opposed to the diagonal cut edge (Fig. 176).

Opening with added or inserted band:
The front garment section is cut in one and has a high necked closing. Mark the centre of the garment with a line of stitching. Make the slash to the right, next to the centre line, or cut a narrow square opening the required length needed to insert band: distance half the width of the band less

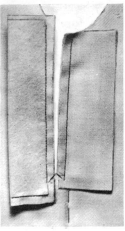
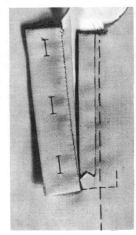

Fig. 177 a   b

Fig. 177

$\frac{5}{8}''$ (1·5 cm) seam allowance. Stiffen the front band with a piece of interfacing, or use the iron-on type of interfacing. Make bound buttonholes, if indicated on the pattern. With right sides together, fold band in half and stitch across lower edge (Fig. 177 a). Do not stitch the lower edge if the band is to be inserted. With right sides facing, baste the front band to the right side of the opening on the outside of garment. Baste the underlap to the left side. Stitch along the length of the opening. Clip seam allowance close to the line of stitching. Press open underlap seam allowance, fold underlap in half and hem to the inside of the garment (Fig. 177 b). To insert band, stitch the lower edge of the band to the square cut edge of the opening. Before turning facing to inside, grade seam allowance, press towards band and hem facing to seam line (Fig. 177).

Neckline Finishes

Shaped facing is used to finish the raw edges of a round, square or V neckline. Cut the shaped facing 1″ to 1½″ (2·5 to 4 cm) wide and on the same grain as the edge it is to finish.

For neckline edges on garments, which are cut on the bias, it is better to cut the facing on the straight grain, as this will prevent the stretching of the neckline edge (Fig. 178).

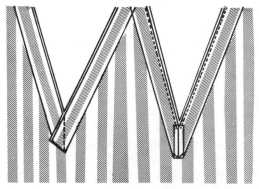

Fig. 178

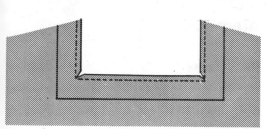

Fig. 179

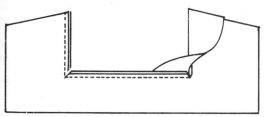

Fig. 180

Decoration and highlighting of the neckline. For a more decorative effect, facing can be of a contrasting colour to the garment. Top-stitch facing with Gütermann Sew-all thread or Gütermann Twist. depending on material thickness, at an even width to the outside of the garment. Start by stitching the right side of the facing to the wrong side of the garment. Turn facing to right side, stitch in position by hand with a slip-stitch or top-stitch by machine (Figs. 179 and 180).

Square neckline: Clip the seam allowance diagonally to the corners.

Rounded neckline (Fig. 181): Baste facing to a round neckline, taking care not to stretch neck edge. For a better fit, and to prevent stretching, cut a piece of interfacing according to the neck facing pattern. Baste interfacing to wrong side of garment. Apply and stitch facing to neckline with right sides together. Trim interfacing close to seamline. Grade seam allowance of facing and clip, especially the curved edges at intervals. Turn facing to inside, baste close to folded edge and place a row of stitching very close along folded edge of neckline.

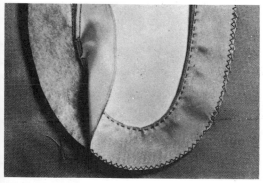

Fig. 181

For more elegant dresses, hand stitch along folded neckline edge. Turn and stitch outer edge of facing, tack facing to shoulder seam and darts. With loosely woven fabrics, facings can be tacked to inside of garment with a few herring-bone stitches.

Needle and Thread Chart

Types of fabrics	Gütermann thread	Machine Needle Sizes	
		Metric	Singer
Bed and table linen, Cotton	Sew-all	70	11
Bed and table linen, Linen, tickings	Sew-all	90	14
Blended fabrics	Sew-all	80	12
Blended fabrics—for hand-worked buttonholes	Twist	100–110	16–18
Cotton, plain and mercerised	Sew-all	70–90	11–14
Curtains, rayon, cotton, wool, linen, etc.	Sew-all	80	12
Curtains, synthetic	Sew-all	80	12
Decorative stitching (coarse)	Twist	100–110	16–18
Decorative stitching, fine, by hand	Sew-all	80–90	12–14
Foulard, blended with synthetics	Sew-all	70–90	11–14
Heavy coating, thick winter fabrics	Twist	100–110	16–18
Lace curtain, cotton	Sew-all	70–90	11
Lace curtain, synthetic	Sew-all	70–90	11
Marquisette, cotton	Sew-all	70–90	11
Marquisette, synthetic	Sew-all	70–90	11
Non-iron cotton	Sew-all	70–90	11–14
Plastic materials, light-weight	Sew-all	80	12
Plastic materials, medium weight	Sew-all	90	14
Poplin, blended with synthetics	Sew-all	70–90	11–14

Needle and Thread Chart

Types of fabrics	Gütermann thread	Machine Needle Sizes	
		Metric	Singer
Poplin, light-weight, made from cotton	Sew-all	70–90	11–14
Silk, light-weight, elegant	Sew-all	70–90	11–14
Synthetic material, Polyester, Nylon, etc., light-weight	Sew-all	70	11
Synthetic material, Polyester, Nylon, etc.	Sew-all	70–90	11–14
Taffeta, plain finish with surface sheen	Sew-all	70–90	11–14
Taffeta, synthetic or blended	Sew-all	70–90	11–14
Toile, light-weight	Sew-all	70–90	11–14
Tropical, light-weight aerated	Sew-all	70–90	11–14
Tropical, synthetic	Sew-all	70–90	11–14
Underwear, Cotton, Rayon	Sew-all	70	11
Underwear, synthetics	Sew-all	70–90	11–14
"Wash and wear" fabrics Synthetic, light-weight	Sew-all	70–90	11–14
"Wash and wear" fabrics for hand-worked buttonholes	Twist	100–110	16–18
Woollen fabric	Sew-all	70	11
Woollen fabric—for hand-worked buttonholes	Twist	100–110	16–18
Worsteds, light-weight medium coating	Sew-all	90	14
Worsteds, for hand-worked buttonholes	Twist	100–110	16–18

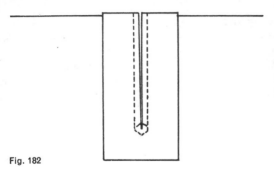

Fig. 182

Fig. 183

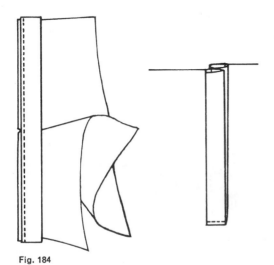

Fig. 184

Openings

Faced openings: Mark the position of the opening on the wrong side of the fabric. Baste a strip of fabric about 1½″ to 2″ (4 to 5 cm) wide with right sides facing to the garment opening line. The lower edge of the facing should be at least 1″ (2·5 cm) longer than the slit. Machine-stitch with Gütermann Sew-all thread, down each side of the line of marking, tapering to a point at the lower end. Cut the slit between the stitched lines and clip diagonally on both sides of the point (Fig. 182). Turn the facing inside and tack to the garment. By hand or machine, stitch close to and all round the edge for a good finish and to strengthen the opening.

Bound opening with bias strip. Cut a slit in the fabric and stitch the bias strip to the opening with right sides together. Stretch the bias strip a little around the end of the slit, so that it will lie flat. Turn the binding inside and slip-stitch to the garment, or machine-stitch with Gütermann Sew-all thread to seam line (Fig. 183).

Bound opening with fabric strip cut on the straight grain, with selvage edge along one side. The fabric strip should be about 1½″ (4 cm) wide. Stitch the cutting edge of the fabric strip in a continuous line to opening edge, right sides together. Fold the strip across the width in the centre and hem the selvage inside garment to the seam line, or machine-stitch to the first line of stitching. Press the binding of the front edge opening to inside and attach with a few stitches to the upper edge. Make a row of stitching through all thicknesses at the base of the strip (Fig. 184).

Opening in a narrow seam: For the underlap, cut a bias strip about 2″ (5 cm) wide, stitch to back edge of opening, right sides together. Press open seam. Fold bias strip through centre and slip-stitch

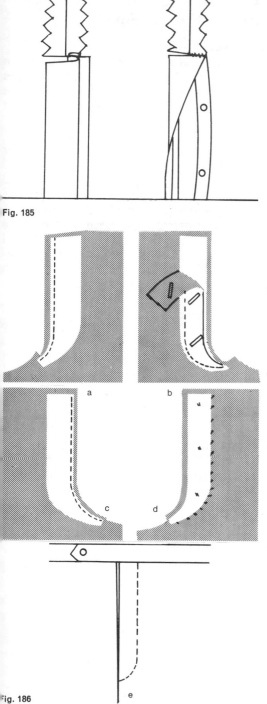

Fig. 185

Fig. 186

over the seam line. For the overlap cut a $1\frac{1}{2}''$ (4 cm) wide bias strip and stitch to front edge opening, right sides together. Turn inside and slip-stitch to garment (Fig. 185).

Fly front for trousers: Face the overlapping side of the left trouser section with a piece of lining. Stitch facing with Gütermann Sew-all thread to opening edge, right sides together. Clip curve down to crotch seam. Turn facing inside (Fig. 186 a) (for fly-zip see SLACKS page 117 and ZIP FASTENER page 135).

For the fly piece, place fabric and lining with right sides facing, stitch on the hollow edge and across the top. Turn right side out. Work diagonal buttonholes according to pattern. Baste fly to the overlapping side of the left trouser section. To prevent fly edge from protruding, place fly $\frac{1}{8}''$ (3 mm) back from front edge. Attach to garment by machining on the fitting line. For a neat finish, push the raw edge of the fly between the top cloth and the lining of the front closing (Fig. 186 b).

Attach fly between buttonholes to front edge with a few stitches, this will keep both edges flat.

For the underlap of the right trouser section, seam lining to fabric with right sides facing. Turn right side out. Stitch the underlap to the right trouser section, through fabric only. The raw edge of the lining may be attached by hand, or turn under raw edge of lining and stitch to seam line. Strengthen the bottom of the fly with a bar tack (Figs. 186 c and d).

Sew small buttons to the underlap. Fig. 186 e shows a correctly worked fly opening.

Order of assembling different kinds of Garments

General
After cutting the fabric, finish each piece separately. Pin together, baste. Press lightly over seams, this will give a better picture when fitting garment for the first time.

Transfer pinned adjustments to the other side. Baste.

Stitch seams, keeping stitching close to basting thread. If possible stitch the seams of several garment pieces in one go, this is more economical. Neaten seams and darts as each line of stitching is completed. This is easier to carry out when garment is not yet assembled.

Press open seams.

Skirt
Stitch all darts. Make pleats, stitch pleats.

Join skirt sections, leave opening on left side or centre back.

Put in zip fastener.

Leave slits at both sides of the skirt lining. Turn up hem. Attach a piece of the skirt fabric to the lining for the underlay (see DIOR SLIT, page 33).

Attach lining to skirt.

Stitch waistband to skirt.

Turn up hem. Hem a pleated skirt before putting in pleats.

Blouse
Stitch darts in front of bodice.

Make the neck opening.

Close side and shoulder seams with a plain seam.

Finish off seam allowance.

Complete collar and join to neckline. Complete sleeves, cuffs and shirt cuffs separately. Stitch sleeves into armholes.

Narrowly hem the lower edge of the blouse. For overblouses make a wide hem and slip-stitch to garment.

Make worked buttonholes. Sew on buttons.

Dress

For a two-piece jumper dress, the process is the same as for skirt and blouse.

A joined dress consists of skirt and blouse. The skirt and bodice unit is joined at the waistline and the dressmaking process is similar.

Interface the front edge. Make bound buttonholes in the right front edge of the bodice.

According to the pattern make pleats and apply the pockets.

Close shoulder and side seams, if necessary leave part of the seam open for the fastening.

Complete the collar and attach to the neckline, or finish the neckline with a shaped facing.

Close the sleeve seams. Finish the lower edge of the sleeve, or apply cuffs to sleeve edge. Sew the sleeve into the armhole.

Sew on buttons. Put in zip fastener. Turn up hem.

Slacks

Work as described on page 117. (See also POCKETS page 97 and OPENINGS page 78).

Jackets and coats

Make the darts in the front sections of garment.

Interface front edges.

Make piped or bound buttonholes. Apply facings and finish buttonholes.

Insert pockets.

Close shoulder and side seams. Ease back shoulder seam.

Interface collar. Join sleeve sections.

Interface sleeve hem, turn the sleeve hem to inside, attach with herring-bone stitches.

Attach collar to neckline. Sew in sleeves.

Turn up hem of coat or jacket. Sew hem into place.

Put in lining. Sew on buttons.

Join fur pieces and attach to coat or jacket.

Children's clothing

Work the same as adult clothing.

Allow 1″ to 1¼″ (2·5 to 3 cm) for the seams. Make hems with two wide turnings, or make tucks around the skirt.

Cut the bodice 1¾″ (4 cm) longer at waistline.

These extra allowances are useful when alterations become necessary.

Allow more material at waistline and lower edge of trouser legs when cutting trousers. Pull up trousers with braces and make wide hems at the lower edge of the trouser leg. Trousers can be let out quite easily later on, especially as children's waistlines do not change all that much, providing that the trousers are not made skin tight.

Hints for alterations

Gathering on skirts or bodice is easily let out. Smocking can be undone on both sides of the bodice or skirt, leaving a group of pleating in the centre of the dress only.

Arrange pleats with less depth, or press the pleats open on both sides of the skirt, so that the fabric lies smoothly and without pleating over hips.

Enlarge the bodice and shoulder section in a plain coloured dress by inserting embroidered braid or other trimmings. Cut through the front and back of bodice, from centre of shoulder downwards.

Widen sleeves by cutting through the centre of the sleeve, from sleeve cap to the lower edge and set in strips of fabric. Set in bands of fabric round the sleeve if lengthening is required.

To lengthen a garment, make a false hem, or trim the edge of the hemline with a strip of fabric in a contrasting colour.

Slacks can be lengthened by knitting a wide waistband and bands round the ankles.

Insert bands at trouser sides for added width.

Fig. 187

Overblouse

This is a loose blouse. The width is gathered in the waistband or elastic is inserted into the lower edge of the blouse underneath the waistline over the hips (Fig. 187).

Overlap and Underlap

Part of an opening that is either lapped over or under another section. The centre of the overlap and the underlap must correspond with the centre of the garment (Fig. 188).

Work the overlap and the underlap in double thickness of fabric. For extra strengthening use interfacing. Make the buttonholes in the overlap and sew the buttons to the underlap. See also NECK OPENINGS, page 72.

Fig. 188

Padding Stitch

Pad stitching is used to join interfacing or canvas to the fabric. For suits and coats, attach the interfacing with padding stitches using Gütermann Sew-all thread, to cuffs, collars and front facings. Hold the fabric and the interfacing in your left hand, so that the right side of the fabric lies over the index finger and the thumb is positioned on top of the interfacing. While pad stitching roll the work over the fingers of the left hand to give it the required shape. Start pad stitching from the crease line of the lapels and work parallel rows. With the needle in a horizontal position, take a stitch through the interfacing picking up only a few threads of the garment fabric. Work the diagonal stitches in parallel rows upwards and downwards. Pad stitching makes the underlayer of fabric contract to shape the roll of the lapel or collar (Fig. 189).

Fig. 189

Fig. 190

Fig. 191

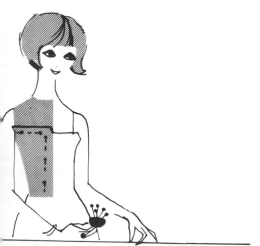

Fig. 192

For **collars,** join the interfacing or canvas to the under collar section and pad-stitch by hand in the manner shown in Fig. 190, or machine-stitch (Fig. 191).

Pattern Adjustments

Each pattern is made according to standard body sizes, and you have to make a few adjustments to accurately fit your individual measurement. Therefore it is best to try on the pattern on your own dress form, or check personal measurements against pattern tissue. Adjust where necessary making certain that allowance for ease has been included. Make the necessary adjustments on pattern, before it is placed on the fabric for cutting.

If the right and left sides of the garment are not identical, pattern pieces for both sides are given. Pin both sides together and try on. Pin pattern pieces to back and front at the centre of your slip. Now you can see where to make the necessary adjustments (Fig. 192).

Place a strip of paper underneath the pattern pieces and pin them so that they touch each other, join darts and sleeve edges the same way (Fig. 193). Now you can try pattern over the left side of your body.

The adjustment for a pattern which is too long or too wide is easier to determine than a pattern which is too small. It is therefore recommended to buy, if possible, a pattern exactly to your body measurement or one size larger.

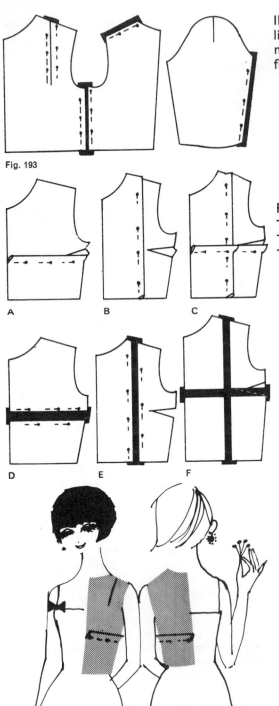

Illustrations opposite show in simplified lines the adjustments which might be necessary for small, slim, large and full figures.

Fig. 193

For small figures:
To shorten: by crosswise fold (A)
To tighten: by vertical tuck (B)
To decrease: combine both (C)

For large figures:
To lengthen: Insert a strip of paper (D)
To widen: insert a vertical strip of paper (E)
To enlarge: use both (F)

The pattern for front bodice is longer at the waistline and at the side seams than your own measurements. The illustration opposite also shows the back view of the bodice; here the pattern bulged above the waistline.

Adjustment (Fig. 194):
Fold an adequate pleat underneath the armhole. At the same time fold a pleat at the same height at the back of bodice. Straighten the centre line at front and back.

Fig. 194

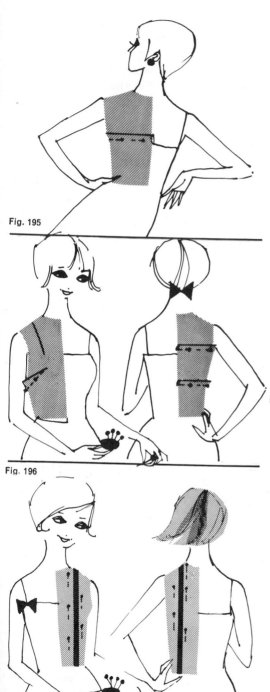

Fig. 195

Fig. 196

Fig. 197

Pattern bulges across shoulder blades:
This is caused by an erect posture.

Adjustment (Fig. 195):
Here one also shortens the pattern by folding a crosswise pleat. Always fold a straight pleat, as pattern pieces have to lie flat on fabric for cutting. The pleat must not shorten the sideseams, therefore it is placed straight across the shoulder blades. As this will decrease the armhole at the back, one has also to reduce the size of the sleeve cap, either by slashing top of sleeve cap and overlapping slashed edges or by tapering the seamline at the top of the sleeve.

Stocky, but plump figure: This type of figure is more often than not short-waisted in the back and long-waisted in the front.

Adjustment (Fig. 196):
An underarm bust dart is necessary for this type of figure. When the length of the front pattern piece is not sufficient, fasten a piece of tissue paper to the lower edge of front bodice. To shorten the back, fold two pleats straight across the pattern, if need be enlarge the armhole a little. Cut out waistline towards centre for about $\frac{3}{4}$" (2 cm) at front of skirt. For exceptionally large figures, enlarge pattern pieces by inserting a vertical strip of paper. If you want to decrease the size, remove about $\frac{1}{4}$" (6 mm) at front and back centre. To enlarge size add $\frac{1}{4}$" (6 mm).

Bust size larger than pattern
Adjustment (Fig. 197):
Slash pattern vertically and increase to desired measurement by placing a strip of paper underneath. This will increase the shoulder dart. After pattern alteration, check width at waistline and shoulder for possible corrections. The width at shoulder is seldom to be adjusted, simply redraw shoulder seam according to the old cutting line.

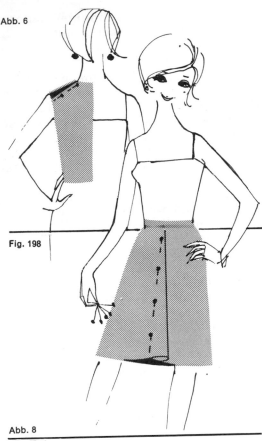

Abb. 6

Fig. 198

Abb. 8

Fig. 199

Square shoulders
Adjustment (Fig. 198):
Open shoulder seam of pattern, starting at armhole edge, insert a strip of paper, enough to obtain a flat shoulder shape and to make it fit smoothly.

You may often find that adjustments have to be made after the garment has been basted. It is therefore recommended to cut shoulder seams with a generous seam allowance.

How to adjust pattern for a gored skirt into a pattern for a slightly flared skirt
Adjustment (Fig. 199):
Pin at front centre a wedge-shaped pleat, which widens towards hemline.

Adjust resulting unevenness at hemline and waistline edge by taping pieces of paper underneath.

Pattern adjustments according to your measurements: Pattern adjustments can be made by trying on the paper pattern or by comparing pattern measurements with your measurements. The latter will give, with some practice, even better results. First of all it is necessary to take your own measurements with a tape measure. Now take the corresponding measurements on your pattern. Compare both measurements. Now you can see whether you need to make any alterations in your pattern.

When comparing pattern and your body measurements, remember, that every pattern has been given an 'ease' allowance. The amount of ease depends upon the design and material. Ease allowance is necessary for the comfortable fit of the garment. Here is an example:

Fig. 200

Garment wrinkles across the back of neckline (Fig. 200).

How do body and pattern measurements compare?

Example No. 1:

	Pattern measurement	Body measurement
Back waist length	16½″ (42 cm)	16½″ (42 cm)
Armhole length	13½″ (34·5 cm)	15″ (38 cm)

Measure the armhole length by pressing a ruler or a book horizontally under the armpit, now measure from upper edge of ruler over and around top of shoulder.

To determine the armhole length on your pattern, place ruler starting at the lower edge of armhole seamline across the pattern ending at the top of armhole seamline.

Body and pattern measurements correspond, but add 1½″ (4 cm) to the shoulder seam of pattern for especially straight shoulders. A shoulder pad has a similar effect.

Adjustment (Fig. 201):
Add ¾″ (2 cm) at the front and ¾″ (2 cm) at back shoulder seam, or insert an adequate strip of paper.

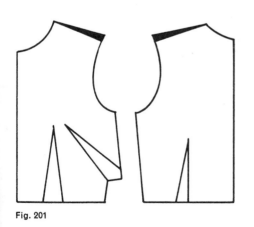

Fig. 201

Example No. 2:

	Body measurement	Pattern measurement
Back waist length	15¾″ (40 cm)	16½″ (42 cm)
Armhole length	13½″ (34·5 cm)	13½″ (34·5 cm)

Here the shoulder is also squarer than shown on the pattern. The length of the

Fig. 202

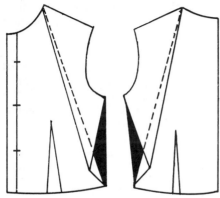

Fig. 203

Fig. 204

armholes is the same, but your back waist length is $\frac{3}{4}''$ (2 cm) shorter than the pattern.

Adjustment (Fig. 202):
Lower both neckline points for $\frac{3}{4}''$ (2 cm) in a straight downward line. Mark the new position of the neckline points, the new lowered neckline and tapered shoulder line. Compare measurements once again.

Shaping to your body contours.

Left and right side of body is not identical: Pattern fits perfectly on one side, but the armhole length and bodice side seam length is shorter on the other side. This side will sag. With a one-sided sloping shoulder line, you will sometimes find a crease forming at the waistline and a protruding hip line.

Adjustment (Fig. 203):
According to your measurements fold a pleat on bodice from outer corner of waistline to neckline point in order to adjust the sagging shoulder-line. Adjust side seam allowance. Increase the hip line allowance on skirt.

Round shoulders.

Adjustment (Fig. 204):
Cut into back of bodice from neckline point downwards to the centre of shoulder blades, make an adequate fold at armhole. This slash will automatically enlarge the neckline. When fitting the garment, make short darts towards the centre in order to restore neckline measurement. It may be necessary to adjust back waist length and armhole length.

Larger than average bust.

Adjustment (Fig. 205):
Cut out dart at front of bodice. Slash pattern front $3''-3\frac{1}{2}''$ (8 to 9 cm) below neckline, straight across to armhole edge. Spread the slash the amount needed to lengthen bodice, but not more than $\frac{3}{4}''$ (2 cm). Taper

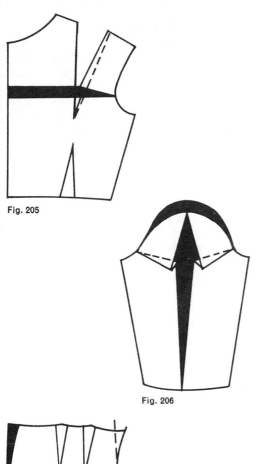

Fig. 205

Fig. 206

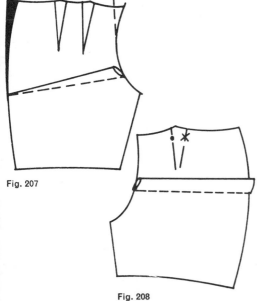

Fig. 207

Fig. 208

the slash towards armhole. Even out the dart line. Dart has now become longer.

Large upper arm: If the sleeve is to be enlarged, the width of the sleeve cap will automatically increase, but this is not always desired, especially if the size of the armhole is to remain the same.

Adjustment (Fig. 206):
Slash sleeve pattern in a vertical line from top of sleeve to the lower edge. Spread the pattern, increasing sleeve at the fullest part by the necessary amount. Pattern pieces touch each other at the top and bottom of sleeve, fold two wedge-shaped pleats from slash to the sleeve cap. Now re-shape the sleeve cap to the original curve. For this purpose, trace on paper outline of sleeve cap before enlarging the sleeve.

Well-fitting slacks: Slacks are often cut too long at the back, i.e. too high at the waist. Slacks should fit comfortably when sitting down, but often a tight fit across the seat is desired for standing.

Adjustment (Fig. 207):
Starting at the centre back seam of slacks, make a wedge-shaped pleat, shift the position of the crease. Adjust the in-creased hipline and remove width at the centre back seam.

Small seat: The depth of crotch (in a sitting position measure the distance from waistline to the chair) is sometimes larger but usually smaller than the pattern.

Adjustment (Fig. 208):
Shorten the pattern at back and front by folding a pleat of equal width straight across.

Permanent Pleating and Machine Pleating

These are pleats pressed into the fabric by machine (Fig. 209). The amount of fabric required should be three times the hip measurement for box and knife pleats. Before sending your fabric away to have it commercially pleated, complete all the seams except for one. Also complete the hem beforehand. If you want to use less fabric, choose groups of pleats with spaces in between (six or eight pleats, leave a space, followed by another group of six or eight pleats, etc.).

Sunray or accordion pleats are tiny, narrow folded pleats at the top of the skirt that widen towards the hemline. For this type of pleating, fabric should be cut in a semi- or full circle, but ask the firm where the material is to be machine-pleated for advice beforehand.

The graceful, swinging width of a pleated skirt made from georgette can be attractively highlighted with a ribbon stitched round the entire hemline. See also PLEATED SKIRTS (page 94) and PLEATS (page 96).

Pin-fit

In order to get an overall picture of how a garment is going to look, pin and assemble all the pieces together. All articles of clothing should be basted together, except for underwear, nightgowns, etc. Modern sewing machines make basting for underwear seams unnecessary. Stitch over pins at right angles to seam line.

Piped Edge

A narrow strip of fabric in a contrasting colour projects from the edge of the garment like piping. The strip of fabric can be attached to the garment edge permanently or may be only tacked to the edge.

Fig. 209

Fig. 210

Cut a bias strip the desired width. With right sides facing, stitch bias strip to the edge of the garment. Press seam allowance towards the garment. The piping is extended to the desired width and turned to inside. Slip-stitch raw edges into place (Fig. 210).

Piping

A folded strip of bias fabric, ribbon or leather is inserted in a seam to form a decorative trimming. This can either be done in a contrasting colour, or in a fabric of different texture.

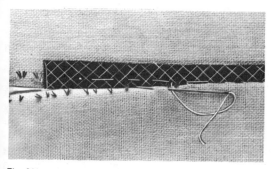

Fig. 211

For a piped seam, cut a bias strip about $1\frac{1}{4}''$ (3 cm) wide. With wrong sides together, fold the strip in half lengthwise. Press with an iron along the fold line. Baste the strip of fabric, ribbon, etc. to the right side of one section of the fabric, with both seam allowances of piping facing towards the seam allowance of the fabric section (Fig. 211).

The width of the piping depends on you, but it is usual for the piping fold to extend for about $\frac{1}{16}''$ to $\frac{1}{4}''$ (1.5 to 6 mm) beyond the seam line. To ensure an even piping, turn under seam allowance of second fabric section and slip-stitch with right sides together to piping seam line. Stitch seam on the inside. Instead of using flat piping, a piece of cording may be encased inside the bias strip. Piping is best done with the edge stitcher attachment of your sewing machine.

Fig. 212

For plain washable fabrics, baste bias strip as described above to one fabric section with right sides together. Turn in seam allowance of the second fabric section and machine-stitch with Gütermann Sew-all thread about $\frac{1}{8}''$ (3 mm) or less from piping fold line to the right side of the garment (Fig. 212).

Braid piping see BRAID, page 13.

Piping is also used to finish the edge of a garment.

Plastic, how to sew

Plastic materials are joined with plain seams, but very rarely hemmed. Do not pin or baste, as pin marks remain visible.

Place two pieces with right sides together and with one seam allowance wider than the other, hold in place with Sellotape. After seam has been stitched, trim the edges to an even width and remove Sellotape.

The presser foot will slide more easily if the surface of the material is lightly dabbed with sewing machine oil. If you wish to sew any quantity of plastic materials, it would be better to invest in a special presser foot attachment with a built-in wheel, then oiling is not necessary (Fig. 213).

Fig. 213

Pleated Skirts

The amount of fabric needed can be calculated according to the waist and hip measurements.

The illustration opposite shows the different kinds of pleating (Fig. 214). A special effect is created when joining pleats using two contrasting colours.

How to calculate the amount of fabric needed for a skirt with side pleats (Fig. 215).

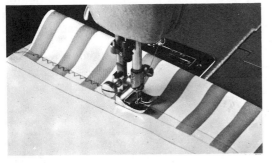

Fig. 214

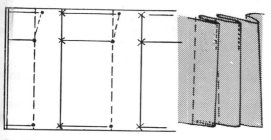

Fig. 215

Example:

Hip measurement (38″/96 cm)+ease allowance (2″/5 cm)=40″/100 cm.

Pleat width (2″/5 cm)+pleat depth (double pleat width 4″/10 cm)=6″/15 cm.

Total hip measurement (40″/100 cm):
Pleat width (2″/5 cm), therefore number of pleats=20.

Number of pleats=20.
Pleat width+pleat depth=6″/15 cm, therefore length of material=20×6″/20×15 cm=120″/3 m.

Waist measurement (30″/80 cm):
Number of pleats 20, therefore width of pleat at waist=$1\frac{1}{2}$″/4 cm.

Pleated skirts should be hemmed before pleats are made.

Place the fabric on an ironing board. Begin with half the depth of a pleat+$\frac{1}{2}$″ (1 cm) seam allowance, continue to pin each pleat, 2″ (5 cm) for width and 4″ (10 cm) for depth, at the top and at the lower edge of the skirt, to the ironing board. Press pleats lightly into position over the pins. Now taper the pleats to waistline measurements. Using a damp cloth, press pleats permanently.

Taper each pleat from the waistline from $1\frac{1}{2}$″ (4 cm) towards the hipline to 2″ (5 cm). The creased edges of the pleats must always be on the straight grain of the fabric. To fit pleated skirt at the waistline, deepen the underside of the pleat and taper pleats to waistline. Join the separate pieces of the fabric together which shouid be 120″ (3 m) and have the width of the length of the skirt+seam allowance+hem.

Skirt with inverted or box pleats, which are top-stitched from waist to hipline:
Calculated according to hip measure-

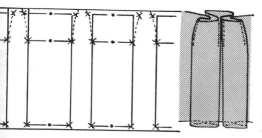

g. 216

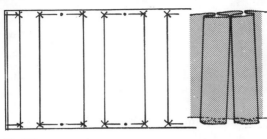

Fig. 217

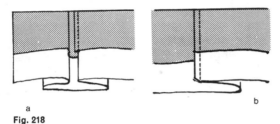

a   b
Fig. 218

ments, pleats are tapered to waistline (Fig. 216 on previous page).

Skirt with unpressed pleats: Here the calculation is based on the waistline measurements; this is only possible when the difference in the measurement between the waist and the hip is small (Fig. 217).

Hem with seamed pleat: Mark the position of the hem at the seam allowance. Clip the seam allowance. Press seam allowance open inside the hem. Turn up and hem to the skirt (Fig. 218 a).

Trim the seam allowance above the hem and make a line of stitching close to the raw edges of the seam allowance (Fig. 218 b).

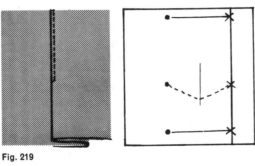

Fig. 219

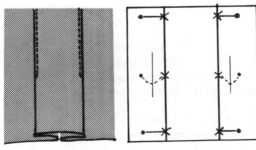

Fig. 220

Pleats

Pleats are used to give fullness and greater movement to certain parts of the garment.

Side or knife pleat: The folded edges of this type of pleat are turned in one direction. They are usually top-stitched close to the creased edge from the waist to the fullest part of the hip. To allow more room for walking in a very narrow skirt, fold pleat from right to left, at the centre back of the skirt. To secure the top of the pleat stitch a curved line to the inside of the pleat, to prevent pleat from tearing (see the curved dotted line in Fig. 219).

Box pleat: Box pleats are two knife pleats, which turn in opposite directions to form a panel. At the inside of the garment both creased edges meet. Box pleats can also be top-stitched and the top of the pleats can be secured from the inside with a curved line of stitching (Fig. 220).

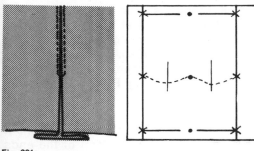

Fig. 221

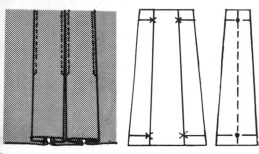

Fig. 222

Inverted pleat: This is a box pleat in reverse. The two knife pleats turn towards each other on the right side, forming a panel on the inside of the garment. Top-stitch close to the creased edge, to the desired length, or they can be sewn together at the inside of the pleat. This type of pleat should also be secured from the inside with a curved line of stitching (Fig. 221).

Pleats which are joined together, taper towards the waistline and give a flared look to the skirt.

To join pleats, cut only half of the inside section on each side of the pleat. Cut the two missing sides of the inside pleat and stitch them with right sides together to the already cut section. This will hold pleats in place (Fig. 222).

See INVERTED PLEAT WITH UNDER-LAY (page 62).

Pockets

Fig. 223

If patch pockets made from light-weight materials are applied to the right side of the garment, interface the fabric for the pocket first. Baste the interfacing over the fabric, line the pocket and slip-stitch to the garment. For more casual clothes, top-stitch patch pocket in position. When using heavy fabrics, it is better to hand-stitch the lining to the pocket (Fig. 223). Stitch the pocket in position with Gütermann Sew-all thread, the desired distance from the edge. Fasten thread ends securely.

Welt pocket: For the welt pocket (Fig. 224 a–c), fold the garment fabric over the interfacing for the welt, attach with herring-bone stitches at the back. Press welt and baste right sides together to the lower line of marking for opening. Baste pocket section to the upper line of marking. This

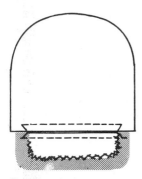

Fig. 224 a

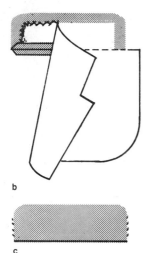

b

c

pocket section should be cut $\frac{1}{2}''$ (1 cm) wider than the pocket opening. Machine pocket lining section and welt with Gütermann Sew-all thread. Make the upper stitching line $\frac{1}{8}''$ (3 mm) shorter than the lower line of stitching. Fasten thread ends securely.

Cut the opening through the garment fabric only, to within $\frac{1}{2}''$ (1 cm) of the ends of the seams. Cut diagonally into the corners, thus forming triangular ends (Fig. 224 a).

Draw the pocket piece through the opening to the wrong side of the garment. Turn up welt and press over opening. Press open welt seam. The second pocket section, which is cut in one with the welt section, is slip-stitched to the right side of the welt. Draw the second pocket section through the opening to inside of garment. Sew to pressed open welt seam, taking care that stitches do not show on the right side of the garment (Fig. 224 b).

On the right side, slip-stitch with tiny stitches the seamed edges of the welt to the garment (Fig. 224 c). Finally stitch the first pocket section to the second pocket section.

Flap pocket: Flap pockets are worked in a similar way. First line the underside of the flap. Place the raw edges of the flap above the marked opening, right sides together (Fig. 225 a). Baste one of the pocket sections below the marking for the opening. Stitch round the marked position of pocket opening. Slash between lines of stitching. Draw the pocket piece through the opening to wrong side. Machine- or hand-stitch across lower edge of opening, close to the seam line. Press flap section down. Press seam allowance up. On wrong side of garment, baste the second pocket section over the first section. Stitch the second piece to flap

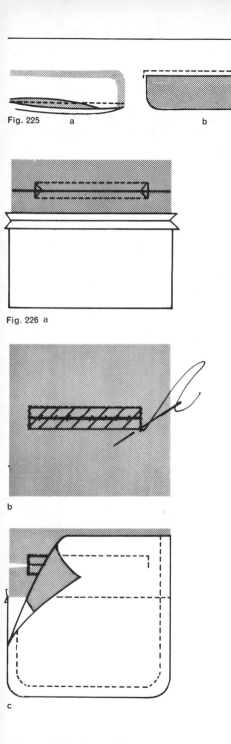

Fig. 225   a   b

Fig. 226 a

b

c

d

seam line, then stitch pocket pieces together (Fig. 225 *b*).

Bound or piped pocket: Baste mark the position of the pocket opening on the right side of the garment (Fig. 226 *a–d*). Cut on bias two strips of fabric. Baste the 2″ (5 cm) wide bias strips along the marking for the opening, on right side of garment. Machine with Gütermann Sew-all thread. Fasten thread ends securely. Stitch one pocket section to the lower edge of the binding (Fig. 226 *a*).

Back pocket section: If the pocket section is cut from lining fabric, it is necessary to face pocket section with a piece of garment fabric. Cut a piece of fabric about 2″ to 2½″ (5 to 6 cm) wide, and sew to the upper part of the pocket (this is to prevent lining showing through pocket opening). Slash through the centre of marking, stopping about ½″ (1 cm) from ends. Clip diagonally into corners, thus forming small fabric triangles. Carefully press seams open. Pull the pocket section and binding through the opening to the wrong side.

Binding must be of uniform width on both sides of the slash. Oversew on binding using Gütermann Sew-all thread to binding seam line. If heavy fabric is used, hold binding in place by machine-stitching along binding seam line. Push the triangles at both ends with needle to inside and slip-stitch into place (Fig. 226 *b*).

Close the edges of the pocket opening with herring-bone stitches. Lay the second pocket section, the one faced with a piece of garment fabric over the first section, stitch to upper edge and ends of binding. Cutting edge of binding and the cutting edge of the pocket must lie exactly over one another, with the faced pocket section over the opening (Fig. 226 *c*).

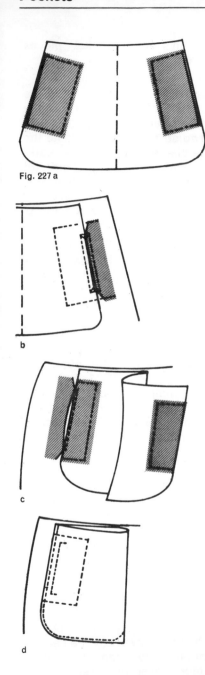

Fig. 227 a

b

c

d

On the right side of the garment, stitch around pocket opening, close to binding, attaching the second pocket section to the first at the same time. Finally stitch pockets together. For a neat finish overcast raw edges (Fig. 226 d).

Trouser pockets: The pocket pouch made from lining material is faced at the inner edges of opening with 2″ (5 cm) wide strips of fabric. On the narrow sides, each strip should be 1″ (2·5 cm) longer than the marking for the pocket opening (Fig. 227 a).

With right sides facing, apply a piece of binding about 1¼″ (3 cm) wide on one side of pocket fitting line. Lay the edge of the pocket pouch opposite binding. Edge of pocket pouch and binding meet on line of marking for opening. Stitch ⅛″ (3 mm) each side of marking and across ends. Slash between stitching to within ½″ (1 cm) of the ends. Clip diagonally into corners, leaving a triangle at each end (Fig. 227 b).

Pull the binding and pocket pouch through the opening to the wrong side. The folded edges will form even bindings along each side of pocket opening. To prevent binding from slipping, machine-stitch with Gütermann Sew-all thread along seam line. The pocket pouch is folded in half only after the front seam line has been stitched. Catch the second pocket pouch edge when stitching along binding seam line at the side. Close both pocket edges completely and finish raw edges (Figs. 227 c and d).

Front hip pockets: Stitch one pocket section to right side of trouser front, right sides facing, top-stitch opening edge of pocket (Fig. 228 a), after turning pocket section to wrong side.

The second pocket section is cut in one with the side section of the trousers. Lap front over side section and baste. On the

Fig. 228   a   b

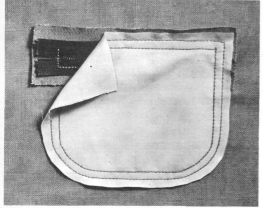

Fig. 229

Fig. 230

right side of the garment, stitch seam at curved edge to form pockets (Fig. 228 *b*). If desired, pocket bags can be left hanging loose. Side seams and waistline seam are enough to hold both sections together.

Pocket closed with Zip Fastener

The pocket opening is bound with a bias strip as described under the heading bound buttonholes. Herring-bone-stitch the edges of the binding together. Baste the zip fastener to the wrong side of the pocket opening. Machine-stitch zip fastener to the lower edge of the binding. Stitch one pocket section to the lower edge of the binding on the inside of the garment. Lay the second pocket section over the first and baste to garment. Stitch second section to the upper edge and ends of binding, then stitch both pocket sections together (Fig. 229).

Pompons

Ready-made pompons can rarely be bought in the size and colour you require.

Cut two cardboard circles and make a hole in the centre. The width of the circle equals half the width of the pompon thickness. Cover cardboard tightly with wool. Cut around the edges and carefully separate cardboard circles and tie a piece of wool firmly round the strands between. Cut the circle open on one side and ease out pompon. Roll the pompon between your hands and fluff up by holding it over steam (Fig. 230).

Princess Style

Coats and dresses in this style are cut in panels which run the full length of the dress or coat from shoulder to hemline.

Fig. 231

The skirt widens into fullness at the bottom. It is a design suitable for the fuller figure (Fig. 231).

Proportion

It is necessary to recognise any figure irregularities. Try to choose a style that will emphasise your good points and draw attention away from other parts. A few basic rules have been given elsewhere, see FASHION HINTS page 40.

Proportional faults like a flat bust can be corrected with a padded bra. A long-line bra will flatten a bulging midriff. If your waistline is too generous, wear a high-waisted elastic girdle.

Use a firm fitting corset if too-ample proportions of hips and seat need to be controlled. A figure with plump thighs need not necessarily have heavy hips, a long-legged pantie girdle is therefore the best solution. Your undergarments like bra, corset, girdle, etc. can do much to create a well-proportioned figure.

Protecting Strips

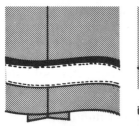
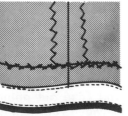

Fig. 232

To prevent the lower edge of trouser legs from fraying sew on a piece of ribbon about $\frac{1}{8}''$ (3 mm) above the fold line. Stitch the protecting strip to trousers before turning up hem, using Gütermann Sew-all thread (Fig. 232).

Raglan

The raglan sleeve is cut in a yoke-like fashion and extends along the shoulder (Fig. 233).

The method used to make raglan sleeves is explained under the heading SLEEVES page 121.

Fig. 233

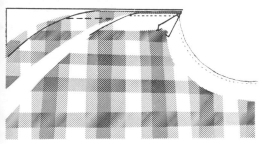

Fig. 234

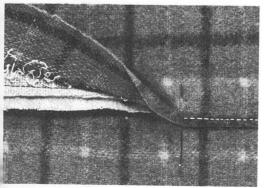

Fig. 235

Raw Edge Finish

The cutting edges of a fabric section are called raw or free edges. When the raw edge of a seam is to be finished with bias band or rayon braid, the facing is basted to the garment section with wrong sides together. Baste the bias band or rayon braid to the raw edge on the right side of the garment and machine-stitch with Gütermann Sew-all thread (Fig. 234).

Reversible or Double Cloth

Double cloth or 'double-faced' fabrics are two layers of material interwoven together by a special process, so that both sides look different.

Seams: Separate the two layers of fabric for about $1\frac{1}{2}''$ (4 cm) along the raw edge. With right sides of one of the layers together stitch a plain seam. Trim and grade seam allowance. Trim away one raw edge side of fabric layer on the underside. Turn under the untrimmed layer of fabric and top-stitch over the first seam enclosing the trimmed edges of same. This row of stitching has a decorative effect on the reverse side (Fig. 235).

Edges: Edges cannot be finished in the usual way. Separate the raw edges for about $1\frac{1}{2}''$ (4 cm). Insert a bias strip, folded in half, to inside where fold is going to be and fasten with a catch stitch. Turn both raw edges inward and slip-stitch (Fig. 236).

Ric-rac

Ric-rac is a wave-like woven braid, which comes in different shapes, colours and strengths. It is often used as a decorative trim on children's dresses.

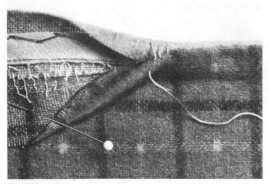

Fig. 236

Stitch braid to garment through the centre or attach to garment with an embroidery stitch, catching each point of the braid (Fig. 237).

For a very attractive effect, apply ric-rac of different widths, fill the spaces with decorative stitch in Gütermann Twist for a wide and colourful border (Fig. 238). See also BRAID page 13.

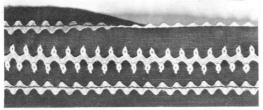

Fig. 237

Right Sides Together

This is an expression used when placing two fabric sections together with the right sides of the fabric facing each other.

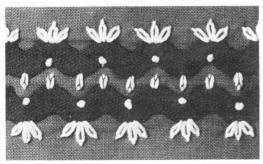

Fig. 238

Rolled Hem

This type of hem is used on delicate fabrics like chiffon, voile, georgette, etc. Roll the fabric edge between the thumb and index finger of your left hand and hem into position with a fine whipping stitch. Keep thread loose (Fig. 239). For best results on such fine fabrics—use Gütermann Sew-all thread.

Even more inconspicuous is a slip-stitched rolled hem. Roll the edge about $\frac{1}{8}''$ (3 mm) between the thumb and index finger and slip-stitch into position. Take a stitch below the rolled hem, then take a stitch through the rolled edge of the fabric. Bring needle out and pick up a few threads below the rolled hem, continue in this manner (Fig. 240).

Rolled hems may also be executed by machine. Using the hemming foot attachment of your machine, the edge of the fabric is folded narrowly over and then oversewn with zigzag stitching. Loosen needle thread tension slightly.

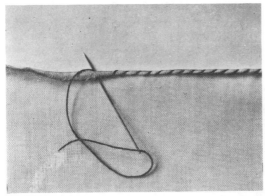

Fig. 239

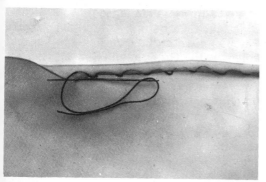

Fig. 240

Ruching

A very attractive method of making a frilly edging suitable for use on children's dresses.

Gathered ruching: Take a narrow strip of fabric or ribbon. Hem or roll-hem the lengthwise edges of the fabric strip. Run a gathering thread through the centre of the fabric strip and draw up. Baste to garment and machine-stitch along the line of the gathering stitches (Fig. 241).

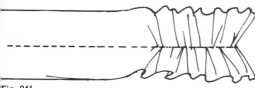

Fig. 241

Shell-gathered ruching: Cut a 2″ (5 cm) wide bias strip. Fold in half lengthwise and baste together, turn inside out, forming a length of tubing $\frac{3}{4}$″ (2 cm) wide. On the back of the tubing insert running stitches, diagonally from edge to edge with Gütermann Sew-all thread (double thread may be used). Take the stitches right within the edges. Draw up the thread carefully to form shells of equal size (Fig. 242).

Fig. 242

The heart-shaped ruche consists of two parts. First cut a 2″ (5 cm) wide fabric strip. Using Gütermann Sew-all thread finish the edges with a closely set zigzag or satin stitch. Fold the strip into pleats and machine-stitch through the centre (Fig. 243).

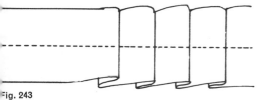

Fig. 243

For the heart-shaped piece, make a length of tubing as already described. Both edges of the tubing are held together with a few stitches and folded into triangles at that point. With the needle pick up a few fabric threads in the centre of the tubing, bring needle back to the first set of stitches and oversew once more with a couple of stitches, using Gütermann Sew-all thread. Repeat the whole process at an even distance of $\frac{1}{2}$″ (1 cm) (Fig. 244).

Fig. 244

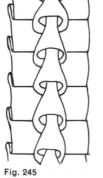

Fig. 245

The completed ruche is slip-stitched to the centre of the pleated ruche (Fig. 245).

Fig. 246

Rose ruching is made from two 2″ (5 cm) wide fabric strips in a contrasting colour. Place the two strips over one another and stitch with Gütermann Sew-all thread. Keep the line of stitching $\frac{1}{4}$″ (6 mm) below the edges. Fray both edges to line of stitching. Form box pleats at an even width of $1\frac{1}{2}$″ (4 cm) and stitch through the centre. The edges of the uppermost pleat are held together with a few stitches at the centre (Fig. 246).

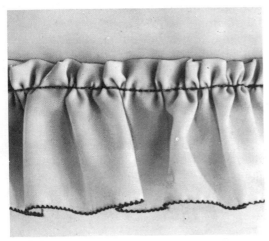

Fig. 247

Ruffles

Ruffles are made from light-weight fabrics. Finish one edge of a strip of fabric, which is cut on the lengthwise grain, with a zigzag stitch or make a rolled hem using Gütermann Sew-all thread. Turn under the upper edge of the strip of fabric, the desired width of the heading plus a seam allowance. Make a row of gathers at the depth of the heading. Stitch the ruffle to the already finished raw edge of the fabric (Fig. 247).

For a fuller ruffle, allow three times more fabric than the edge to which it is applied. Allow only two and a half times more fabric, if a slightly stiffer fabric is used.

Ruffles cut on the bias of the fabric: Fold the bias strip in half, wrong sides together. Close to the cutting edge, make a row of gathers. Baste ruffles edge to edge with right sides together to the garment. The ruffle is held in place with a bias strip (Fig. 248). Stitch one edge of the bias strip over the seam line of the gathered edge of the ruffle. Turn bias over the edges, baste in place and hem to the fabric (Fig. 249).

Fig. 248

On transparent fabric, the bias strip encloses the trimmed seam allowance.

Ruffles with facing: These are used to decorate collars on children's dresses and

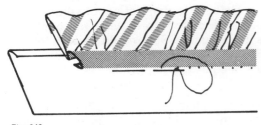

Fig. 249

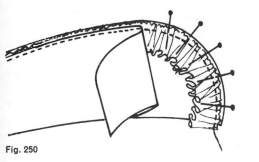

Fig. 250

Fig. 251

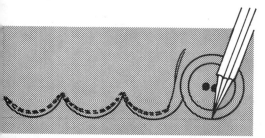

Fig. 252

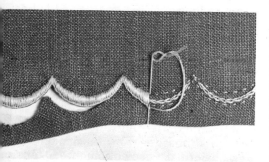

ig. 253

capes. Ruffles are basted to the edge of the upper collar section, right sides together, allowing for more fullness at corners. Baste under collar section or facing over the ruffles. Stitch the seam through all thicknesses and turn facing to wrong side (Fig. 250).

Circular ruffles: These are ring-shaped fabric sections. Cut the circle open on the straight grain. Sew the ruffle pieces together. Finish the lower edge of the ruffle with a narrow stitched or rolled hem. Circular ruffles are not gathered. Baste and stitch the ruffle in place among the seam line on the garment. Circular ruffles cut from taffeta retain an even width, whereas softer fabrics should be left to hang for a certain time before the final cutting.

Saddle Stitch

This decorative hand stitch is used to outline collars, pockets or the edges of a closing. It is best done in a contrasting colour with Gütermann Twist. Stitches must be of even length, and each stitch must be longer than the space between them, however not longer than $\frac{3}{8}''$ (1 cm) (Fig. 251). This stitch is also used for making leather gloves.

Scalloped Edge

Use a close blanket stitch to edge scallops. Mark the outline of the scallops with a scallop gauge, a coin or a button. Scallops worked on light-weight materials, should be underlaid with a piece of the same fabric (Fig. 252). This is not necessary if a heavy-weight fabric is used. Fill the scallop edge with a chain stitch. Work blanket stitch over the chain stitch, keeping stitches close together (Fig. 253). When completed, trim away fabric close to

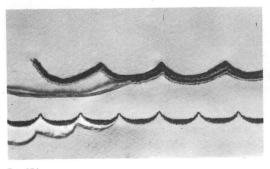

Fig. 254

scallops with a pair of sharp scissors, taking care not to damage the embroidered edges.

Scalloped edges made by machine: The simplest forms are small scallops made by machine, using an embroidery attachment (Fig. 254 bottom).

For large scallops, draw the contours on to your fabric. Machine-embroider the outlines with a close zigzag stitch. Make one more line of zigzag stitching over an inserted thread which is carried along underneath. The points of the scallop edges must interlock. Place a thread along the scallop edges and, using a small zigzag stitch, embroider once more over the edges, and over the thread to give a slightly raised effect (Fig. 254 top).

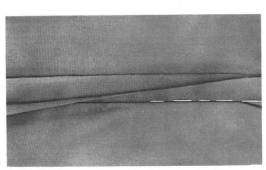

Fig. 255

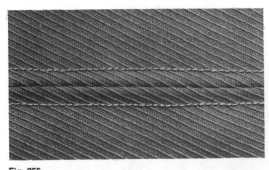

Fig. 256

Seams

A plain seam is used to join two fabric sections together. Baste two pieces of fabric with right sides together and stitch a seam close to basting thread with Gütermann Sew-all thread. Press the seam open (Fig. 255).

Double top-stitched seam: This is often used as a decorative finish on garments. This type of seam gives a flat appearance with added stiffness to the pressed open seam allowance of coarse and heavy fabrics (Fig. 256). Press open seam allowance. Press only lightly over the seam, so that the raised effect is maintained. Each row of stitching should be at an equal distance of about $\frac{1}{8}''$ to $\frac{1}{4}''$ (3 to 6 mm) on either side of the seam line. Use the longest stitch setting on your machine. Wind Gütermann Twist onto the bobbin. Place the work face down on the machine and sew as normal. Ease bobbin thread tension slightly and tighten the upper thread tension.

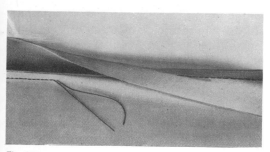

Fig. 257

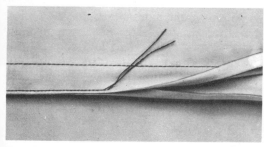

Fig. 258

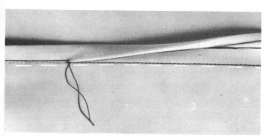

Fig. 259

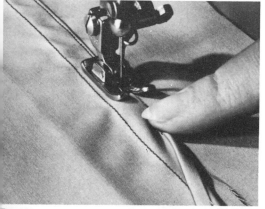

Fig. 260

French or double seam: Fabric sections are placed with wrong sides together. Make a plain seam. Turn the fabric and press flat at the seam line. Pin the fabric sections with right sides together and stitch a second seam, encasing the raw edge of the first seam. The finished seam should be neat and no thread ends should be visible (Fig. 257).

Mock French seam: This seam is similar in appearance to the French seam. First stitch a plain seam, with right sides of the fabric together, seam allowance should be about $\frac{3}{4}''$ (2 cm) wide. Turn the raw edges of the seam allowance towards the centre seam line. With folded edges meeting, stitch them together, close to the folded edge (Fig. 258).

Standing fell seam: Baste fabric layers together, so that the lower layer projects about $\frac{1}{4}''$ (6 mm). Make a plain seam. Turn under the raw edge of the lower layer and fold over, thus enclosing the shorter seam allowance. Stitch close to the seam line. This seam can be executed in one process. This is a strong ridged seam (Fig. 259).

Run and fell seam: Stitch a plain seam with right sides of the fabric together. Trim the seam allowance of upper fabric layer to about $\frac{1}{4}''$ (6 mm), fold the lower seam allowance over the trimmed edge. Stitch close to the folded edge. Place the fabric section flat on your machine and stitch with ordinary presser foot (Fig. 260).

Work is made easier, if your sewing machine has a special edge stitcher. This attachment serves as a guide to ensure accurate stitching on the edge of the fabric as it encases both raw edges.

Slot seam: This is a decorative seam. Press open the wide seam allowance of a basted seam. A strip of fabric is placed

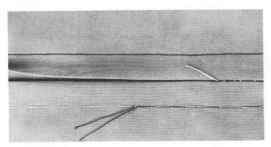

Fig. 261

under the seam allowance, to the wrong side of the fabric. Top-stitch on the right side of the fabric at an equal distance from each side of the basted centre seam line with Gütermann Sew-all thread. Remove basting thread, press under a damp cloth (Fig. 261).

Fig. 262

Top-stitched seam: This is a strong seam and at the same time adds a decorative effect to the garment. Stitch a plain seam. Press both seam allowances to one side. Top-stitch with Gütermann Sew-all thread on the right side of the fabric, at an even distance close to the seam line (Fig. 262).

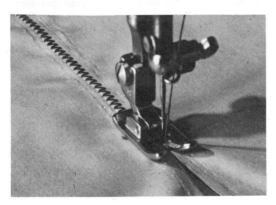

Fig. 263

Edge to edge seam: This type of seam can be used, when the selvages of two fabric sections adjoin, i.e. the piecing together of bed linen or linings. Place selvages close to each other and oversew with a zigzag stitch, so that the needle locks both edges alternately (Fig. 263).

Seam Finishes

Before finishing the raw edges of a seam, cut off any loose threads and press seam open.

A quick and accurate method to finish cutting edges is to use zigzag stitching. The length of the zigzag stitch depends on the type of fabric being used. Use a close stitch setting for firmly woven fabrics and a longer stitch setting for loosely woven fabrics (Fig. 264).

Fig. 264

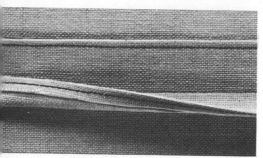

Fig. 265

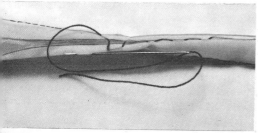

Fig. 266

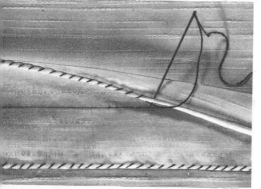

g. 267

Place the seam allowance under the presser foot so that stitches lock alternately in the fabric and just outside the fabric edge. Thread tension should not be too tight or edges tend to pucker.

For fabrics that unravel easily, it is better to turn and stitch the edges. Fold under the raw edges and machine-stitch close to the folded edge. Trim and press open. Ridges should not show on the right side of the garment after pressing (Fig. 265).

Note: Place a strip of brown paper between the seam allowance and the wrong side of the fabric; this will prevent seam imprints showing through.

Another method of finishing a seam, is to stitch the raw edges against one another. For sheer fabrics, turn the edges to inside and slip-stitch together (Fig. 266).

For firm crepe fabrics, trim seam allowance to $\frac{1}{4}''$ (6 mm) and stitch both edges together with zigzag stitches.

As the selvage of chiffon is more firmly woven than the actual fabric itself, and will pucker more easily when stitched, it is advisable to cut off selvage in order to obtain a more supple seam. Finish either by turning under the raw edges or neaten the raw edge of the seam allowance.

Rolled edges make a neat seam finish on delicate and transparent fabrics. Roll the seam allowance between the thumb and the index finger of your left hand to a narrow fold of about $\frac{1}{4}''$ (6 mm). Oversew the rolled edge with tiny whipping stitches using Gütermann Sew-all thread (Fig. 267).

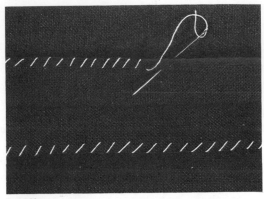
Fig. 268

Oversewing is the best method for a neat seam finish. Press seam open and oversew the edges with small stitches. Do not pull thread too tightly, otherwise edges will turn under (Fig. 268).

For fabrics that are firmly woven and do not unravel, trim the edges with pinking shears. If pinking shears are not at hand, use a pair of sharp and pointed scissors. Cut into the edge in one direction and then once more in the opposite direction, thus forming an angle.

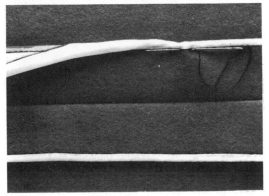
Fig. 269

The bound edge seam finish is best used in jackets or coats if they are unlined. Encase each raw edge of the seam with bias seam binding or braid. With right sides together, stitch one edge of the binding close to the raw edge of the seam. Fold binding or braid over to the wrong side of the seam allowance, attach with running stitches along the seam line. The free edge of the binding will disappear under the open pressed seam (Fig. 269).

If braid is used, fold in half lengthwise and press. Place the raw edge between the folded braid and hand-stitch through the upper braid edge, the raw edge and the lower braid edge with Gütermann Sew-all thread (Fig. 270).

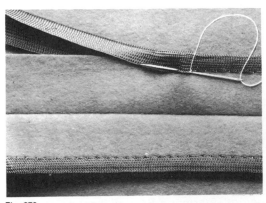
Fig. 270

Selvages

Selvages are lengthwise borders on both sides of the fabric. As they are more firmly woven than the actual fabric, it is advisable to cut them off before sewing, to prevent the material from puckering at the seams.

One likes to keep selvages on long seams as it makes it unnecessary to finish the otherwise raw edges of the seam, but in this case clip selvage at intervals.

Sewing machine—Causes of faults and their remedies

Heavy turning of machine

Cause	Remedy
Driving belt is too slack and keeps slipping, or belt is too tight and causes too much pressure on bearings. (This applies only to older machines.)	Replace belt or reposition motor.
Machine is dirty because unsuitable oil has been used.	Use only first-class sewing machine oil (never olive oil).

Machine not feeding correctly

Cause	Remedy
Feed dog stands too low and feed teeth do not protrude far enough through throat-plate.	Raise feed dog, so that feed teeth are above needle plate.
Dust and fluff between feed dog and needle plate.	Unscrew needle plate and remove dust.
Not enough pressure on presser foot.	Adjust pressure.
Presser foot sole is damaged or rough.	Polish with emery cloth or replace.

Thread breaks

Cause	Remedy
Incorrect threading.	Check instructions for correct threading.
Wrong needle system is used.	Insert suitable needle. (Correct needle system is usually found in sewing manual or on the machine itself.)
Knot in thread.	Use only the best sewing thread in needle and bobbin.
Thread bits are present in the stitch-forming mechanism.	Remove thread and lint and oil mechanism.
Upper tension too tight.	Adjust tension.
Needle hole damaged by needle.	Polish needle hole with emery cloth or

have it checked by a sewing machine mechanic.

Imperfect stitches

Cause	Remedy
Upper and lower thread not interlocking in the centre of the fabric.	Tension of upper and lower thread should be carefully adjusted.
Needle not accurately set in the needle bar.	Insert needle according to instructions.
Bobbin is not evenly filled.	Wind bobbin evenly according to instructions of sewing manual. Do not wind by hand.
Thread controller spring is bent or broken off.	Should be replaced by qualified mechanic.

Lower thread loops are uneven

Cause	Remedy
Sewing machine is not equipped to handle elastic sewing threads. Brand-new machines sometimes show this kind of fault. Stitch-forming mechanism is not set to use thread made from silk or synthetic fibres.	The after service of the sewing machine makers should check your machine and re-set the stitch-forming mechanism, to enable you to use all known thread brands on the market.

Needle breaks

Cause	Remedy
Needle is bent and caught in the bobbin holder.	Insert a new needle.
Needle is not suitable for thread.	Consult NEEDLE AND THREAD CHART (page 76) for suitable size of needle.
Bobbin holder is clogged with lint, stitch-forming mechanism is jammed, or out of timing.	Should be newly adjusted by qualified mechanic.
Do not pull or remove fabric, otherwise the needle may become bent and strike the throat plate instead of the needle hole.	Guide the fabric lightly. Do not force or pull through the machine.
Bobbin case incorrectly set in bobbin case holder.	Insert bobbin case until it snaps into lock position.

Upper tension too tight.

Adjust tension.

Missing stitches

Cause

Remedy

Needle incorrectly threaded.

Check your instruction manual for correct threading.

Needle is bent, or blunt.

Replace with a new needle.

Needle is not suitable for thread.

See your NEEDLE AND THREAD CHART (page 76) for correct size of needle.

Incorrect setting of bobbin case holder.

Must be adjusted by a sewing machine mechanic.

Needle inserted incorrectly in needle clamp.

Insert needle in needle clamp as far as it will go.

Fig. 271

ig. 272

Shaping

This means moulding a certain garment section into shape by pressing (Fig. 271). Only woollen fabrics can be pressed into a lasting shape. A lesser degree of shaping is achieved with blended fabrics which contain synthetic fibres, and only then if the percentage of woollen fibres predominates.

Shrink and shape the fabric under a damp cloth. In order to retain the shape, woven interfacing is attached to the fabric with padding stitches. Press collars on suits and coats by stretching the edges into shape (Fig. 272).

Long narrow sleeves: To obtain a curved shaping at the elbow, stretch the sleeve seam slightly while pressing.

Shirtwaister

Shirtwaisters have collars, cuffs and are buttoned through. The skirt is of moderate

Fig. 273

width. This type of style can be made into a simple or more elegant dress, depending on the type of material used (Fig. 273).

Shot Fabrics

The iridescent effect is produced by weaving contrasting coloured yarns in warp and weft. Depending on the incidence of light, one of the colours predominates. This property has to be taken into account when cutting the fabric.

Shoulder Pad

Shoulder pads are used to correct figure irregularities or to highlight a prevailing fashion.

Several layers of cotton wool are graduated to make the pad flat on one side and rounded on the other. The semi-circles of cotton wool are sewn together through all thicknesses with diagonal stitches, to hold the padding in place. While stitching, hold the pad in a curved position to give it the desired shape. A light-weight fabric cut on the bias is used to cover the padding. Attach the shoulder pads to shoulder and armhole seam.

Nowadays, shoulder pads can be bought ready-made in several shapes and sizes.

Shrinking Fabric

Most woollen fabrics have been treated for shrinkage. Garments made from fabrics which have not been pre-shrunk will, if treated the following way, keep their shape and can be safely dry-cleaned later.

Steam-press the fabric in its full width under a damp, but not dripping wet, cloth. Let the steam disperse and dry fabric on a flat surface.

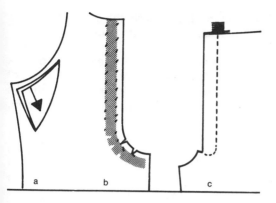

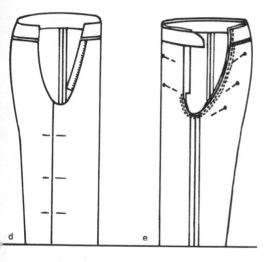

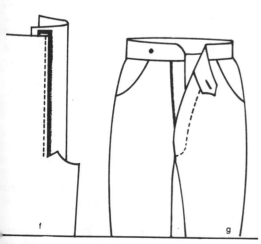

Fig. 274

Large pieces should be shrunk by a dry cleaner.

You don't have to shrink synthetic fabrics, for instance sanforized fabrics are already pre-shrunk.

When fabrics are made from a mixture of synthetics and wool, the treatment depends on the percentage of wool in the mixture. If there is more wool in the fabric steam-pressing is to be recommended.

Cotton and other washables can be shrunk by immersing the fabric in hot water. They have to be ironed before cutting out.

Crepe material should never be shrunk in any way, and is best dry-cleaned.

Slacks

A good pattern, adjusted according to your figure measurements, is essential for slacks and shorts. Make the darts at the waistline and press towards the centre. Reinforce the crotch with a fabric square and place it crosswise against the inside of the front section of the slacks (Fig. 274 *a*).

Front or side closing respectively. On the left front section of the slacks reinforce the appropriate edge with a piece of tape. Sew tape to the wrong side of the fabric (*b*). Turn under edge and stitch over zip fastener so that zipper teeth are covered (*c*).

If slacks have a pocket in the right side, stitch one pocket section with right sides together to the right side of the front section. Again reinforce the seam line of the pocket opening with tape, seam binding or interfacing. The second pocket piece is stitched to the right side of the back section. The second pocket piece

Fig. 275 a   b

should be faced with the same fabric as the slacks. Press seam open.

Join the side seams of one front and back section from the bottom to the lower end of the pocket or side closing respectively. Stitch inner leg seam and press open. When joining sections, match corresponding notches at fabric edges carefully, this prevents the sections from being sewn together back to front (d). Stitch pocket sections together. Baste upper pocket edge against waistline edge.

For the popular slanted pocket, the second pocket piece is cut in one with the yoke-like front section of the slacks (g). For the side closing stitch folded edge of closing over the other side of the zipper tape. You can now attach waistband to each section of the slacks separately; this has the advantage that when at a later stage, adjustments have to be made, the whole of the waistband need not be removed. Baste the two sections of the slacks with right sides together and stitch the centre seam, reinforce with a second row of stitching. Press seam open.

Front closing: Turn under right front edge. Baste over zipper tape close to chain, top-stitch through all thicknesses, including the underlaid fly facing (f). Now fold waistband to inside of slacks and slip-stitch, or if preferred attach the whole of the waistband now. Finish the lower edge of the slacks, or make turn-ups. These types of slacks are shown in Fig. 275 a and b.

Sleeves, the construction of

Before basting sleeves into garment, stitch seams with Gütermann Sew-all thread.

Puffed sleeve: This type of sleeve is the easiest to work and to set in (Fig. 276)

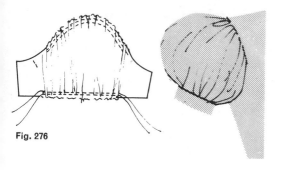

Fig. 276

Place two rows of machine basting between markings of sleeve cap. (Distance between the two rows should be about $\frac{1}{4}$" (6 mm).) Basting stitches should end about $2\frac{1}{2}$" (6 cm) before sleeve seams, in that way fullness is later concentrated around top of sleeve and uncomfortable bulges under the arm can be prevented. Pull up thread until sleeve cap fits armhole. Fasten thread by winding it around a pin. When inserting sleeve in garment match notches in sleeve and armhole.

One-piece sleeve (Fig. 277).

A short and smooth-fitting sleeve should have an adequate width at lower edge. It should not pinch or be too loose.

Three-quarter length sleeve fits better by making short darts at elbow.

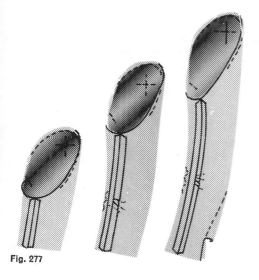

Fig. 277

Long, narrow sleeve: Between notches at elbow height, gather rear seam line slightly and stretch front seam line to match. This will give elbow the necessary ease. Narrow sleeves have a slightly forward curved form when held up. Lower edge of sleeve curves outward so that the edge of the sleeve is longer at the back of the wrist. When arm is bent at right angles, lower edge of sleeve should run in a vertical line.

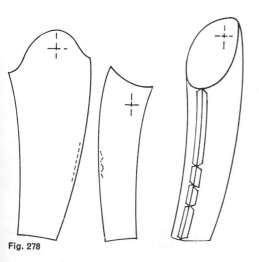

Fig. 278

Two-piece sleeve (Fig. 278): This type of sleeve is mostly used in suits, coats and tailored dresses. Observe markings for shrinking and stretching of fullness at under and upper section of sleeve. Gather fullness slightly between notches with a thread and press under a damp cloth. Sections which have to be stretched should also be pressed under a damp cloth.

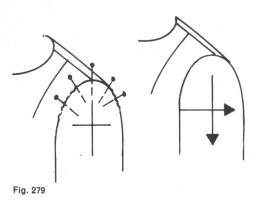

Fig. 279

Fig. 279 a

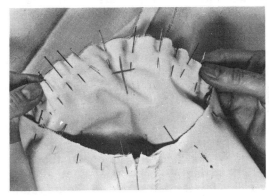

Fig. 280

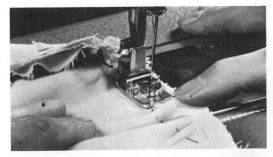

Fig. 281

Sleeves, how to set in garment

Place right sides of sleeve and bodice together and pull sleeve through the armhole. Be careful to match notches, otherwise you will insert the wrong sleeve.

Distribute fullness with no puckers or gathers evenly to both sides of shoulder seam (Fig. 279). Keep about $\frac{3}{4}''$ (2 cm) across top of sleeve smooth (Fig. 279 a). Keep distributed fullness to front of shoulder seam. Keep grain line of sleeve cap straight. Shrink out fullness at back of sleeve cap by pressing seam over a seam roll.

Before you pin sleeve in armhole, ease out fullness by holding sleeve cap at a slight curve. Pin sleeve with pins at right angles to seam line (Fig. 280). Keep underarm section of sleeve smooth.

Sleeves fit better when armhole is not cut too deep and the side seam of bodice comes well up into armpit.

When fitting garment, turn under seam allowance of sleeve cap, pin sleeve over armhole with pins at right angles (Fig. 279). Adjust and steam-press fullness evenly before your next fitting. Baste sleeve in armhole with small stitches. Try on garment once more—if sleeve fits—use Gütermann Sew-all thread to machine-stitch sleeve into armhole with sleeve uppermost on machine, begin stitching at underarm seams.

To avoid puckers and gathers, here are some tips to assist you: Place both index fingers on sleeve and seam allowance in front of presser foot. Pull fabric slightly towards outside and follow sewing with your fingers (Fig. 281). Gathers disappear in the slantwise running fabric, and you can, by following basting thread, stitch a smooth seam over it.

Fig. 282

Fig. 283

Raglan sleeve (Fig. 282): Typical of this sleeve is the slanting, yoke-like and tongue-shaped cut.

There are one-piece raglan sleeves with a shoulder dart and two-piece raglan sleeves.

Stitch dart at top of a one-piece raglan sleeve, taper stitching to a fine point. Stitch the front and back of a two-piece raglan sleeve together, matching notches and markings.

Before inserting sleeve in armhole, reinforce front and back armhole edges of garment by placing sewing tape on the back of fabric in order to prevent stretching. Be careful not to stretch sleeve edges, when basting sleeve in armhole, easing sleeve and garment front to fit. To obtain a flat seam, clip seam allowance, but don't clip sewing tape. Press seam open. Depending on the design, top-stitch close to finished seam on the outside of garment.

Bat-wing sleeves (Fig. 283) are cut in one with the bodice. The great width of the sleeve makes a gusset unnecessary. Grain line on bat-wing sleeves runs diagonally. Slightly stretch bias seam, when machine-stitching. The slant of the front and back of a cut-in-one sleeve are often different from each other. Join the two pieces which have different grain lines, right sides together, pin them to a tailor's dummy so that fabric hangs naturally. This method prevents the forming of diagonal wrinkles at sleeve seam.

Clip curved seam allowance under the arm to prevent seam from stretching (Fig. 283).

Kimono sleeves (Fig. 284) are also cut-in-one with the bodice. A gusset is inserted, when greater freedom is needed in a narrow sleeve.

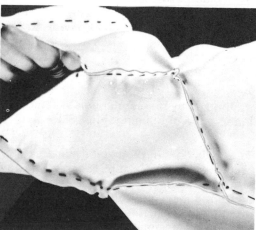

Fig. 284

Semi-kimono sleeves: Here only one section of the sleeve is cut-in-one with the bodice. Either the front or the back section of the sleeve is cut-in-one, whereas the other section is cut with a sleeve cap. A half-gusset is sometimes inserted into the cut-in-one section of sleeve.

Underarm gussets are worked into half or three-quarter length sleeves. These gussets are inconspicuous and give greater comfort in a narrow sleeve (Fig. 284).

Gussets give freedom of movement in cut-in-one sleeves. They are inserted in various ways into the short slashes in the underarm. To prevent corners from fraying, fasten these places securely. To do this, use taffeta or poplin if fabric is heavy, or same fabric if fabric is light. Machine-stitch a bias square over the outside of slash edges. Slash between stitched lines but not through stitching at the point, turn facing to inside of garment, press seam line of facing slightly towards the underside (Fig. 285).

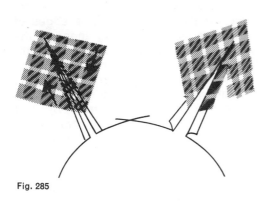

Fig. 285

Stitch underarm seams of bodice and sleeve, turn under seam allowance of gusset opening. Baste gusset opening over bias cut gusset piece, right side up. Turn garment to wrong side, machine-stitch gusset with Gütermann Sew-all thread. Reinforce corners with a reverse back stitch.

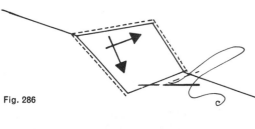

Fig. 286

A somewhat simpler, but more lasting method, is by top-stitching gusset close to faced edge of opening (Fig. 286).

There is a third method; instead of facing corners of slash, oversew the raw edges of slash, press under seam allowance of gusset and top-stitch over gusset opening. This method is very simple, but not as professional in appearance (Fig. 287).

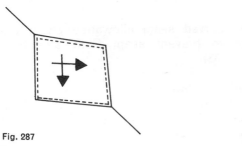

Fig. 287

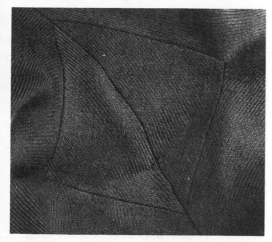

Fig. 288

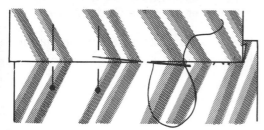

Fig. 289

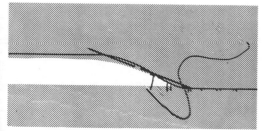

Fig. 290

Two-piece gusset (Fig. 288): Work in the same way as for one-piece gusset. Baste one section of gusset to back of bodice and the second gusset section to front bodice. Stitch underarm seams of bodice and sleeve.

Slip basting

Slip basting is used to match seams in plaid or striped fabrics. Slip baste on the right side of the fabric. Fold under the seam allowance of one fabric edge and pin over the second fabric section, carefully matching fabric design and slip baste together. Slide needle along the fold of the upper section. Bring needle out of fold, pointing it directly down through the lower section, taking a stitch on the wrong side and bring needle back to the right side. Repeat (Fig. 289).

Slip-stitch

A slip-stitch is used to apply trimmings to a garment and to finish hems, when stitching should not show. Work stitches close together (Fig. 290). See also HAND STITCHES, page 54.

Smocking

Smocking is a decorative way to gather folds and is especially used on children's dresses, blouses and nightgowns (Fig. 291).

With this method, gathered pleats are held together with simple embroidery stitches. Mark the pattern on the wrong side of the fabric with evenly-spaced dots. You can use a smocking transfer to iron on the fabric, or use a perforated stencil for the marking of the dots. Smocking is done before the garment is made up. This is necessary because it is difficult to judge

Fig. 291

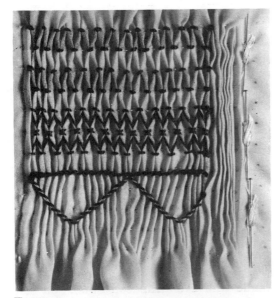

Fig. 292

the different widths of the embroidery stitches beforehand. One usually allows double the width of the material for smocking.

Gather the fabric with a strong thread according to the dotted pattern markings. Pull up the thread and gather the fabric into evenly-spaced folds. Secure the thread at the end of each row by winding it around a pin. Decorative embroidery stitches are worked on the right side of the fabric on top of the folds using Gütermann Twist (Fig. 292).

Round yokes are best worked over a cardboard stencil, which is cut according to the pattern. Baste the gathered fabric section over the cardboard (Fig. 293).

Honeycomb pattern: Draw together two pleats with two back stitches. Carry the thread through the inside of the pleat to the next row either above or below and draw together two more pleats; continue in this manner. Keep the back stitches drawn tight but keep the diagonal stitches at the back of the fabric loose.

Decorative smocking can be worked in horizontal rows, as a zigzag pattern on a yoke edge or may be used to highlight the waistline.

Remove the gathering thread after smocking is completed. Do not press.

Snap Fasteners

Snap fasteners should always be sewn to the double thickness of the fabric, and at least $\frac{1}{4}''$ (6 mm) from the edge of the closing. The ball part is usually sewn to the overlap of the closure. Place a pin through the centre hole of the ball part to the underlap in order to locate the exact position of the socket part of the snap (Fig. 294),

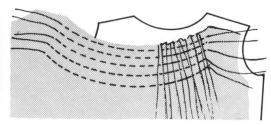

Fig. 293

or rub chalk over the ball, before pressing it against the opposite side. Sew on with Gütermann Sew-all thread, using four to five stitches for each hole. No stitching should be visible on the right side of the garment. Turn the socket part of very small snaps, so that stitches, when pressing snaps together, will not be directly opposite each other.

Spacings

Tucks, rows of top stitching and pleats must be evenly spaced to look effective. They should run the required distance apart and parallel to one another. A hand gauge is useful for measuring and spacing.

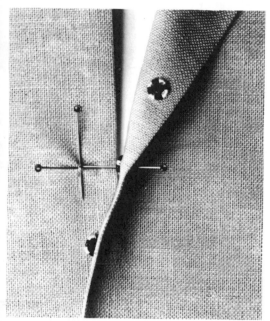

Fig. 294

Stretching of Fabric

The sections which have to be stretched are marked on your pattern. These sections have to be pressed into shape under a damp cloth before basting and sewing (Fig. 295). Place the section which has to be stretched on to your ironing board and, using rotating movements, press with the tip of your iron over the edge of the fabric. To prevent a wavy effect, press slightly over and above the indicated marking. Be careful to determine the exact place where the stretching is needed before you start pressing, as it is impossible to restore the material to its original shape after pressing.

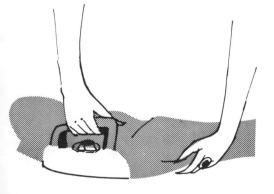

Stiffening and Backing

To give a garment shape and added durability, place interlining or interfacing between the fabric and the lining. It is important to choose the right type of shaping material for your fabric. For synthetic fabrics use a synthetic interlining or interfacing, so that both react the same way when washed or dry-cleaned.

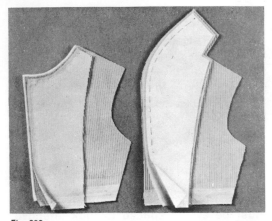

Fig. 296

When using very stretchable light-weight fabrics, mount the whole width of the fabric with organza before cutting. Tack to fabric with diagonal stitches.

For garment sections where seam imprints should not show on the right side, attach the interfacing to the wrong side of the garment section. Stitch the facing to the garment, right sides together. The seam allowance lies between the interfacing and the facing. Clip the seam allowance at intervals and grade seam allowance to eliminate bulk (Fig. 296 left).

Fig. 297

When facings are turned to the outside of a garment, as for instance lapels, baste the facing right sides together, and place the interfacing over it (Fig. 296 right).

Interfacing mitred corners: Herring-bone stitch interfacing to hem fold line on the wrong side of the fabric. The projecting fabric edge is trimmed away diagonally for about $\frac{1}{2}''$ (1 cm) from mitre fold line. Turn under cutting edges and slip-stitch together. Herring-bone stitch hem to interfacing. Line section afterwards (Figs. 297, 298 and 299).

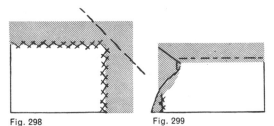

Fig. 298   Fig. 299

Fig. 300

Iron-on interfacing can be used to stiffen front facings, cut-in-one facings and pocket flaps (Fig. 300). The interfacing is cut in the shape of the facing section, so that after the interfacing has been ironed on, the seam along the edge of the interfacing can be executed. Press interfacing to fabric under a slightly damp cloth. Leave for a few minutes to cool before continuing sewing. To remove interfacing, cover with a damp cloth, press with a hot iron and pull off interfacing section immediately.

Stripes and Checks

Special care must be taken when working with materials which have cross stripes or checks with a dominant crosswise direction.

When stripes are unevenly distributed, care must be taken to match the repeat of the same group of stripes, this should be done before the fabric is cut. Baste fabric edges together, carefully matching the design of the fabric (see also SLIP BASTING page 123). Cut the sections carefully and baste the seams, making two rows of basting instead of one: this will ensure that the matched design remains in place after seams have been machine-stitched.

Soutache (or Russia) and Tubular Braid

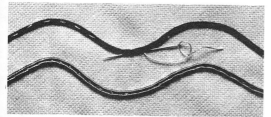

Fig. 301

These are narrow braids. Soutache consists of two narrow tubes covered with a rayon thread. This type of braid is very flexible and can be easily shaped into ornamental designs.

The braid is attached to the fabric with tiny running stitches in the centre between the two tubes. The narrow tubular braid is sewn to the garment either with tiny running stitches in a matching coloured thread or slip-stitched. In this case lift the braid slightly and with a needle pick up only a few threads from the lower side of the braid (Fig. 301).

Tailor's Tacks

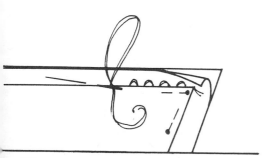

Fig. 302

Transfer all markings on pattern to fabric. Use tailor's tacks for pattern pieces cut from double thickness. Use Gütermann Sew-all thread and if necessary use a contrasting colour. Take a stitch through the pattern along the stitching line and both layers of fabric, take a second stitch

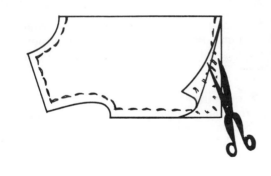

Fig. 303

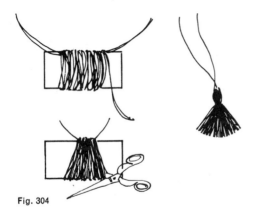

Fig. 304

over the first, leaving a long loop, and continue until all markings have been made (Fig. 302). For darts and assembly dots use contrasting thread.

Check carefully, making certain all necessary markings for assembling the garment have been made, lift pattern carefully from fabric. Pull the two layers of fabric gently apart to full extent of loop and cut the thread between the layers. After you have basted the garment pieces together and before you stitch the seams, remove tufts of thread (Fig. 303).

Tassels

Cut a piece of cardboard the desired length of the tassel. Wind the thread or yarn around the cardboard. Tie a thread through the upper end. Cut through the lower ends. Wrap thread around the upper end of the tassel and secure firmly (Fig. 304). Heavy thread like Gütermann Twist is ideal for this job.

Tools for Dressmaking

Scissors: Use a large pair for heavy fabric, a medium-sized pair for all other kinds of dressmaking, and small, pointed scissors with curved blades to cut open buttonholes and for trimming raw edges, e.g. appliqué.

Needles: Sewing needles in assorted sizes, rustproof steel pins with large coloured heads, a supply of machine needles. A bodkin for inserting ribbons or tape.

A heavy **Pin cushion.**

A **magnet** to pick up scattered pins.

A well-fitting **thimble.**

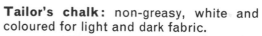

Tailor's chalk: non-greasy, white and coloured for light and dark fabric.

A tape measure with a hole, which can be used for making circles, made from a pliable material.

A **hand gauge** for measuring hems, pleats and spacings. It is quite easy to make one from cardboard.

Threads—see thread chart on page 76.

A **tracing wheel** for marking fabrics.

A short **ruler** and a large **tailor's square** with one edge curved.

A **skirt marker** to chalk-mark hemline yourself without the help of a second person.

An **iron** with thermostat control.

An **ironing board** that is tightly padded and either suited to your height, or adjustable.

A **sleeve board** with an interchangeable and washable cover.

Tailor's ham and seam roll for ironing sleeves and parts which are difficult to press.

Two **pressing cloths,** one linen and one of fine wool.

Most important of all: a **sewing machine.** A sewing machine with an automatic zigzag stitch will not only help you to sew more correctly, but will make your sewing easier.

Top-stitched Seam

Stitch a plain seam. Press both seam

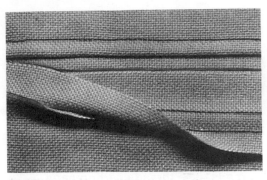

Fig. 305

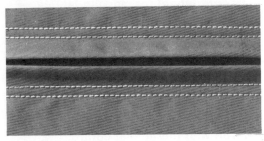

Fig. 306

Fig. 307

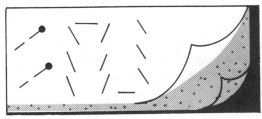

Fig. 308

allowances to one side. On the right side of the garment, stitch close to seam line through pressed seam allowance.

For a raised effect, do not make a plain seam. Turn under one fabric edge, lap over remaining edge, matching the seam edges and top-stitch (Fig. 305).

Top-stitching and Quilting

Top-stitched seams sewn by machine usually consist of several rows of stitching running parallel to each other. Special consideration should be given to the upper and lower (bobbin) thread tension.

Ornamental seams are quickly executed by machine. Use a long stitch setting (loose thread tension). For a raised effect use Gütermann Twist (Figs. 306 and 307). For a special effect, wind two parallel strands of twist onto the bobbin, place the work face-down on the machine and sew as normal, easing bobbin thread tension slightly and tightening the upper thread tension. This will result in a neat, pleasing, double decorative effect.

Quilting: Top cloth, wadding and lining are basted together through all thicknesses. Use a diagonal basting stitch over the whole of the surface (Fig. 308).

Straight quilting designs over a large surface can be quickly and accurately executed with the quilter and guide attachment and the use of Gütermann Sew-all thread. The adjustable guide is especially useful for the even spacing of the parallel rows of stitching (Fig. 309).

Diagonal designs are best worked with a zigzag stitch, as it will preserve the elasticity of the fabric. Quilting is done with a long stitch setting and a loose thread tension.

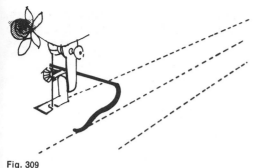

Fig. 309

A very attractive raised effect is obtained by tracing the printed design over a layer of cotton wool wadding by machine.

For a partly quilted surface, stitch the fabric and the lining according to the design. Make a small incision in the lining of the motif and fill with cotton wool. Close the opening with a tiny overhand stitch.

Tracing

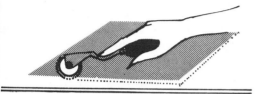

Fig. 310

Tracing is used for transferring markings and construction symbols from pattern to fabric with a tracing wheel (Fig. 310). The saw-tooth edges should not be too sharp or they will tear the fabric.

Tracing with Carbon Paper

See also MARKING OF FABRIC, page 67. For an easy method, use dressmaker's carbon paper to transfer markings from pattern to the fabric.

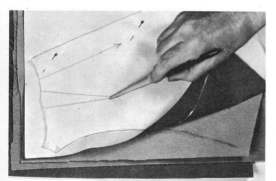

Fig. 311

How to use carbon paper: With two layers of fabric right sides together, put carbon paper with colour side up under lower layer of fabric, place another sheet face down over the upper layer of fabric. The coloured side of the paper is in each case turned towards the wrong side of the fabric. Place pattern over carbon paper, pin all layers together. With the dull edge of a tracing wheel or pencil, transfer all markings to the fabric (Fig. 311).

Trimmings

Strips of fur, velvet or braid may be used for a decorative effect on pockets, collars, cuffs or along the hemline. The separately finished or lined trimming can be applied

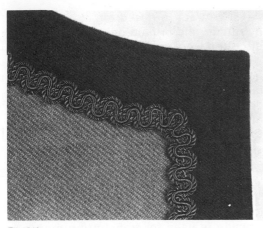

Fig. 312

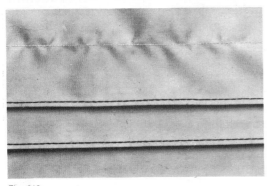

Fig. 313

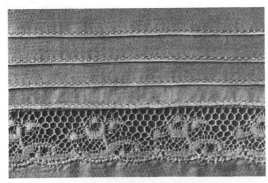

Fig. 314

to the finished garment with a slip-stitch. See SLIP-STITCH (page 123). It can also be used for the edging of garment sections (Fig. 312).

Tucks

Tucks must be worked on the straight grain or diagonal to the grain. Stitch and press tucks before cutting out the garment piece.

Hand tucking is made easier if you pull a thread from your fabric, marking the tuck location. Draw out thread for about $\frac{3}{4}''$ (2 cm), taking care not to break thread. Smooth down fabric (Fig. 313). Make a crease on the tuck line and hand-stitch with a small running stitch close to the crease.

It saves time if you make tucks by machine. Mark tuck location as described and machine-stitch tucks to the required width. (Fig. 314). It is easier still to use the tucker attachment and a twin needle.

To obtain equal spacing between tucks on fabrics with a smooth texture, use a hand gauge. See SPACING (page 125).

Tunics

A tunic is a straight loose-falling top, often extending over hips with only a slight indication of a waistline. Tunics should never fit tightly over hips. Short slits at each side will prevent this.

Turning two fabric layers to right side

This is a method used to join two fabric sections, enclosing the seam allowance, and with the seam lying exactly in the

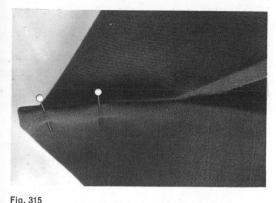

Fig. 315

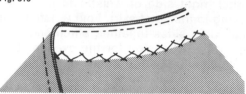

Fig. 316

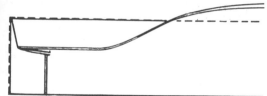

Fig. 317

outer edge, when the sections are turned to the right side (Fig. 315).

The lower free edge of the second section can be hemmed to the garment with herring-bone stitches (Fig. 316).

It is not necessary to trim the corners when using a light-weight fabric. Turn under the lengthwise seam allowance, then turn down the seam allowance at both sides, secure and turn the sections to right side. In this way, turnings lie exactly over one another and fill out the corners (Fig. 317).

This method is recommended for all washable materials, as it prevents corners from fraying.

Trim away corners when using heavy materials. This is particularly necessary in order to eliminate bulk of too many fabric layers. See also COLLARS page 21. Facings, linings, shaped facings and bias strips are attached to the garment in this manner.

Two-piece

This is a garment consisting of two pieces, for instance a dress and a jacket, or a skirt with a jacket (Fig. 318). They are made from the same fabric. A two-piece made from a material of a different kind but harmonising in colour and pattern is called a 'Co-ordinate'.

A suit or an ensemble consists of a dress or skirt with a coat, or a suit with a coat.

Velcro

See BURR OR NYLON HOOK TAPE FASTENER page 16.

Fig. 318

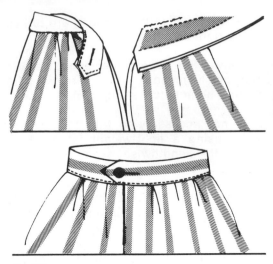

Fig. 319

Waistband for Skirt and Slacks

Cut a piece of fabric on the straight grain, the length of your waist measurement, plus overlap and twice the finished width. Cut the interfacing half the width of the waistband. Insert and stitch interfacing or petersham ribbon close to fold line at the inside of the waistband. If petersham ribbon is used, hold in place with herringbone stitches.

Stitch right side of waistband and interfacing to inside of skirt. Fold waistband in half, right sides together, stitch ends and along the extension for the overlap. Turn waistband inside out. Turn under free edge of waistband and stitch over the seam on right side of skirt. Make buttonholes or attach hooks and eyes (Fig. 319).

For more elegant skirts, stitch interfaced edge of band to the outside of the skirt, right sides together. Fold free edge of waistband to inside of skirt and slip-stitch into place. Close the placket with a zip.

Windcheater

This is a short and comfortable fitting blouse or jacket with a waistband. Collar, cuffs and waistband are often knitted. It is closed at the front with an open end zip fastener (Fig. 320).

Fig. 320

Fig. 321

Zigzag Stitch

A zigzag stitch is used to insert or to join lace, braid or other trimmings. Reduce the stitch length on your machine. This stitch is also used to stitch two edges of fine and transparent fabric together and to finish the raw edges of seams. To prevent the unravelling of a self-fringe, make a line of zigzag stitching just above the pulled thread (Fig. 321).

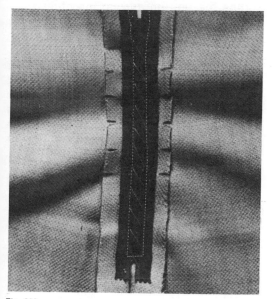

Fig. 322

Zip Fastener

Sewing a zip into a garment is the easiest way to obtain an inconspicuous closing. If the opening for a zip has slightly curved edges (side seam), strengthen the edges on the wrong side of the garment with seam binding tape. Attach the tape along the seam line with herring-bone stitches. Clip seam allowance at intervals (Fig. 322).

Lapped seam application: Baste the whole of the side seam together, including placket opening. Stitch the seam with Gütermann Sew-all thread to the base of the opening. Press the whole seam open and remove basting thread.

The back seam allowance is pushed forward for about $\frac{1}{8}''$ (3 mm) from underneath pressed crease line. Baste edge as close as possible to zipper tape, with fold line touching zip teeth. The zip fastener now lies concealed beneath the closing edge of the front skirt section and is basted to it (Fig. 323).

It is advisable to sew in zip fasteners by hand to begin with, using matching coloured Gütermann Sew-all thread. Make tiny, hardly visible stitches on the right side. Now remove basting thread. Zip fasteners can be sewn in by machine or by hand.

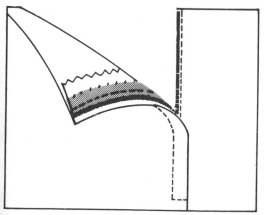

Fig. 323

Do not pull fabric edges too tight when inserting zip fastener, otherwise zip will buckle; ease the fabric when basting to zip.

A matching-coloured zip fastener need not necessarily be concealed. Baste the zip fastener in the opening. Hold edges of opening together with diagonal basting. Using presser foot or zipper foot attachment, machine-stitch down one side, across the bottom and up the other side. Press carefully and remove basting threads.

Zip fasteners that open at the top of a garment, are secured with hooks and eyes. Sew a hook and a thread eye at the top of the opening above the zipper. The hook is sewn to the inside edge of the opening to a piece of tape. Make a thread eye on the opposite side (Fig. 324).

Fig. 324